The Le Mans 24-Hours Race

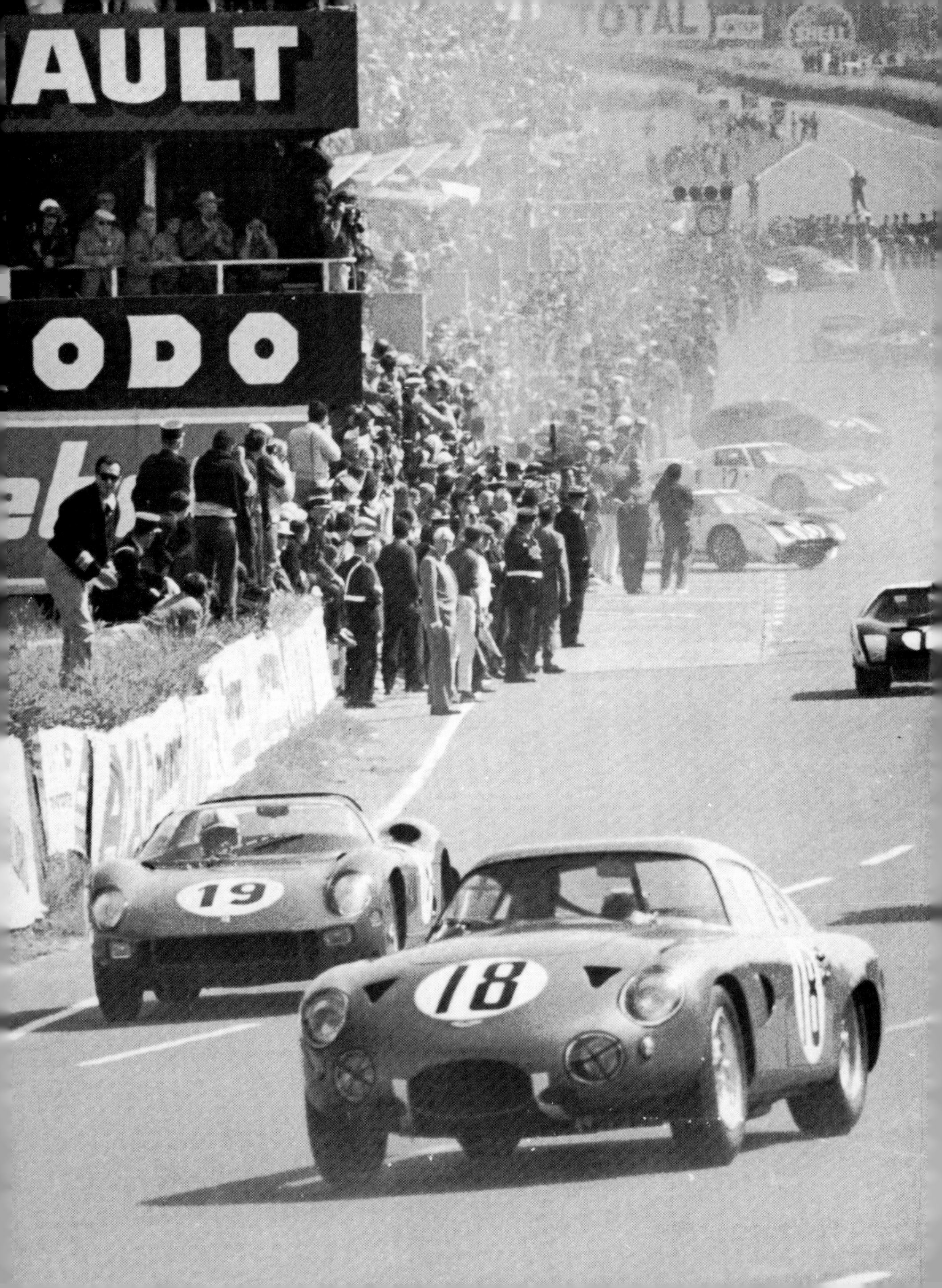
AULT
ODO
TOTAL
19
18
17

THE LE MANS
24-HOURS RACE

Michael Cotton

Patrick Stephens Limited

Front endpaper *Barnato and Rubbin in the winning Bentley, 1928* (BDC) **Rear endpaper** *The winners in 1988, Jaguar beating Porsche by just half a lap* (Jaguar) **Title spread** *The start of the race in 1964, with Mike Salmon leading in the Aston Martin DB4 Zagato. Behind are John Surtees (Ferrari 330P, 19), Berney's Iso Rivolta (1), Parkes' Ferrari 275P (21), and Amon's AC Cobra Daytona (6). The race winning Ferrari 275P of Guichet and Vaccarella (20) is midfield* (Ford).

© Michael Cotton 1989

First published in 1989

British Library Cataloguing in Publication Data

Cotton, Michael, *1938-*
    The Le Mans 24-hours race.
    1. France. Le Mans. Racing cars. Racing. Races : Grand prix d'endurance de vingt-quatre heures de Mans - (Motor race), to 1982
    I. Title 796.7'2

    ISBN 1-85260-091-8

Patrick Stephens Limited is part of the Thorsons Publishing Group, Wellingborough, Northamptonshire, NN8 2RQ, England.

Printed in Great Britain by The Bath Press, Bath, Avon

10 9 8 7 6 5 4 3 2 1

Contents

Acknowledgements

T HE author and the publisher gratefully acknowledge the co-operation of the Automobile Club de l'Ouest in the preparation of this book.

The author would also like to thank the following for their assistance with illustrations: Alfa Romeo, Automobile Club de l'Ouest, *Autosport*, Bentley Drivers' Club, Daimler-Benz, Dunlop, EMKA, Ford, Haymarket Publishing Ltd, Jaguar, Motofoto, Porsche, Renault, Rothmans and Andrew Whyte.

Foreword
by Derek Bell

THE 24-Hours of Le Mans is the world's most famous motor race, and the fact that it can draw up to 50,000 British enthusiasts each year (more than attend the Silverstone or Brands Hatch rounds of the World Sports-Prototype Championship) indicates that it is held in special affection in Britain.

It is a special event for me, as my five successes since 1975 have won me the recognition of being the most successful Briton to compete in the race. I will always be grateful to John Wyer for enabling me to win in 1975, to Porsche AG for providing me with the best car in 1981, 1982, 1986 and 1987, and to Jacky Ickx, Hans Stuck and Al Holbert for helping me to complete my record. I hope, too, that I haven't yet closed my run of successes!

I hope that this book about *Les Vingt-Quatre Heures du Mans* by Michael Cotton will help to widen the popularity of the race still further. It has captured the unique history and atmosphere of the event, and makes good reading.

Author's introduction

T HE sheer power of modern racing cars enables them to exceed 200 mph, momentarily, at a number of European racing circuits yet perversely, their ability to run at speeds greater than those of most private aircraft has forced circuit owners to change the landscapes of their tracks. Gone, now, are the Masta Straight at Spa, and the undulating home stretch at the 'old' Nürburgring, and even the main straight at Monza is punctuated by a second-gear chicane.

For that reason, among many others, Le Mans retains a special attraction for sports car racing followers—the Mulsanne Straight. Here, for a minute on each lap, 700 horsepower Porsches, Jaguars, Mercedes, Nissans and Toyotas reach their peak velocities of up to 240 mph (386 km/h), their slipstreams rattling the gleaming armco steel barriers and rustling the leaves on the trees beyond. At night, bright lights give but a few seconds' warning of the passing of a Group C racing car, the driver of which is making a number of calculations and assessments: the instruments have to be checked, including tyre temperatures and pressures and fuel consumption; the road is bumpy, and it may be necessary to find helpful camber to move across the road to pass a slower car; that slower car may be caught at the 'kink', normally taken without slowing down, or its driver may be about to overtake another.

If the driver is lucky it will be a fine night, but perhaps it will be raining, or misty. Then, wet through, red-eyed, blinded by spray, he'll wish he was anywhere else on earth! All the drivers reach their lowest ebb at dawn, merely half-way through the event and need the morning sun to revive their spirits, and hope rises that the car will reach the finish intact. If the car is in a strong position, worry is compounded by the slightest change in engine note, or imagined reactions to bumps in the road.

The changing faces of the Dunlop Bridge, beyond the pits. **Above left**, *in 1950 as Briggs Cunningham and Phil Walters pose with 'Le Monstre' after finishing eleventh.* **Left**, *the bridge was rebuilt in 1978, and* **above**, *a Jaguar passes by in 1987.*

The event began in a gladiatorial atmosphere, 50 cars and drivers jostling for good positions in the opening laps, but by Sunday afternoon it's a question of survival, and winning. The cars are travel-stained, 'tank-tape' covers bruises on the bodywork, and many are cruising at reduced speeds when, for one reason or another, the drivers have given up hope of winning. Then, success is finishing, claiming a place in the final classification, something for the manufacturers and sponsors to advertise.

In the pits sleep overcomes the mechanics who have been alert all night, but a crackled message from the driver, or from the signallers at Mulsanne Corner, immediately brings them back to life again. Then at four o'clock it's all over . . . one crew has won, 25 perhaps have finished, and 25 more have already started their journeys home. Three drivers mount the balcony of the Automobile Club de l'Ouest to accept garlands and trophies, and to spray champagne on to the throng of well-wishers below, and national anthems make this an emotional moment.

The younger drivers enter for Les Vingt-Quatre Heures du Mans with unalloyed pleasure, glad of the chance to take part in the world's greatest, most famous endurance race. Arguably it is the most prestigious four-wheeled sporting event in the world, though in a different way the annual Indianapolis 500 also makes its claim. Victory brings fame, and Jacky Ickx is the most famous of all competitors with six successes to his credit. Derek Bell, who has won it five times, and Henri Pescarolo, four times, are current competitors, and Olivier Gendebien also won the race four times in the heyday of Ferrari.

Older drivers have learned to respect the Le Mans circuit and its 13.52 km of track (approximately 8.4 miles), much of it public highway where 150 mph (240 km/h) averages are possible. Some vow never to return, knowing the inherent dangers of travelling the 6 km (3.7 mile) Mulsanne Straight 370 times in 24 hours, of passing slower competitors with a differential of 50 mph (80 km/h), and racing on when visibility may be poor, adhesion almost non-existent.

Each year in mid-June Le Mans is a Mecca for up to 50,000 British spectators (more, even, than watch the British rounds of the World Championship for Sports-Prototype cars at Silverstone and Brands Hatch). It is a place for excitement and passion, but also for sightseeing, camp fires, barbecues, tiredness and cold. It is never less than an *experience*!

Le Mans is but one of a dozen Group C sports car championship races contested by major manufacturers, and the cars are unashamed two-seater racing models designed to run at these speeds in relative safety. Their engines are usually based on production versions but need not be, and are tuned to at least 650 horsepower. The sport's governing body, the Federation Internationale du Sport Automobile (FISA), simplified the regulations in 1982, when the Group C formula was evolved, in stipulating a maximum amount of fuel that may be used in the course of the event; at first it was 600 litres per 1,000 kilometres, but this has now been pegged to 510 litres as a way of making the manufacturers more interested in engine efficiency. The Group C.1 cars may not weigh less than 850 kg, nor must they be wider than 2,000 mm or longer than 4,800 mm; further restrictions limit the fuel capacity to 100 litres (and the rate of refuelling to 60 litres per minute), and the size of the 'ground effect' venturi underneath the car, which produces an aerodynamic wing effect in reverse and may download a car to five or six times its static weight, producing amazing cornering power in excess of 2g.

There is another group, C.2 which is specifically for the less experienced, and relatively less wealthy teams. The cars are a little smaller, may weigh as little as 700 kg, and must use no more than 363 litres of fuel per 1,000 kilometres. As in C.1 there is no restriction at all on engine size and a wide variety of power units is seen, including the Cosworth DFL V8, turbocharged four cylinders from Ford, Hart, Zakspeed and Carma FF, and Rover's rally-bred V6. To be truly competitive these engines need to develop at least 400 bhp in race trim, using no more than the allocation of fuel, and in this 'detuned' state they tend to be reliable, if properly prepared.

The C.1 class produces a wide variety of engines: from Porsche, the 911 Turbo's production-based flat-six with twin turbochargers, and around 3 litres in capacity; from Jaguar, the XJ-S/12 V12 non-turbo engine of 7 litres; from Mercedes, a 5 litre V8 with twin turbochargers; from Nissan, a race-designed V8 of 3 litres, with twin turbochargers; from Toyota, a 2 litre, 16-valve four-cylinder engine with a single turbocharger. Although the manufacturers make disparate claims for power outputs, from 650 bhp for Porsche to 730 bhp for Mercedes, lap speeds are so comparable that one must assume about 700 bhp for all of them, when running to the correct fuel economy. When qualifying there is no check of fuel consumption, and with higher boost pressures the turbocharged engines could easily deliver 800 bhp for the critical laps on soft-compound tyres. That, of course, explains why the normally-aspirated Jaguars are usually at a disadvantage in qualifying.

Many people believe that the current breed of sports cars are too far removed from production models, and until 1939 Le Mans was, indeed, specifically for road-going sports cars. The term 'prototypes' only became fashionable in the early post-war years, when few manufacturers had an up-to-date sports car in their catalogues.

Spectacular as they are, there is reason to say that the cars have outgrown the courses, even Le Mans. On the 6 km straight, between the Hunaudières restaurant and the braking area for the acute Mulsanne Corner, they achieve terminal speeds of 1 km/10 sec, or 100 m/sec. The armco barriers have been heightened and reinforced in recent years but the thinking drivers are still extremely uneasy, knowing that in the event of a collision, or bodywork flying off, the car could easily take to the air and end its flight among the trees, with catastrophic results.

The early days were almost leisurely by comparison. Le Mans, the capital of the agricultural Sarthe region of France and 200 km (125 miles) south-west of Paris, had hosted the first Grand Prix de l'ACF in June 1906. A 103 km (64 mile) road circuit was secured to the east of the city and on each of two days competitors had to complete six laps, with an aggregate result. It was won by Ferenc Szisz in a 13 litre Renault (with new Michelin detachable rims, very handy on the unmade roads) at an average speed of 103 km/h (64 mph). Léon Bollée was already established as the Le Mans constructor of touring cars, and in 1907 Wilbur Wright, the American aviator, made his temporary home in the cathedral city, constructing a bi-plane in the Bollée works and using the Hunaudières racecourse (for horses) as his flying strip.

Motor racing took a back seat as the Grand Prix de l'ACF went on tour to other regions, but from 1911 to the outbreak of the Great War a number of important races were held on a shorter, 50 km (30 mile) road circuit to the east of the city. Among these was the first motorcycle race to be held in the Sarthe, first and second places going to the British makes Triumph and Rudge-Whitworth.

Le Mans, therefore, had a sound motor racing tradition to rely on as Europe recovered from the terrible ravages of war. In August 1920 the Coupe Internationale des Voiturettes was organized by the regional club (now, the Automobile Club de l'Ouest) on a course that closely resembles the one in use today, south of the city. At its northern end it came into the suburbs of Le Mans, the drivers taking a hairpin to the right at the Pontlieue crossing, before taking the N138 in the direction of Tours. Before Mulsanne, the competitors turned right on to a D-road in the direction of Arnage, then right again towards Le Mans, and the course measured 17.4 km (approx 10.8 miles).

Although the first Grand Prix, in 1906, had been held in daylight for approximately six hours on each of two days, the public remembered it as a two-day event, and the notion of a 24-hour race was never far from the ACO's thinking. The secretary-general, Georges Durand, arranged a meeting at the Paris Salon de l'Automobile in October 1922, with Charles Faroux, editor of *La Vie Automobile*, and Emile Coquille, the French distributor for Rudge-Whitworth; the company made automobile parts, including lighting, and when Faroux suggested holding a race that lasted for 24 hours, Coquille offered to put up the Rudge-Whitworth cup and the sum of 100,000 francs (none of which was paid to the competitors, mind, a precedent that would last for many years!). Durand was the driving force who gained the permission of the ACF and the authorities needed to close public roads.

Originally the Rudge-Whitworth Cup was a triennial award. Those competitors who completed the 24-hour duration in May 1923 would be invited to race again in 1924, and the successful teams would be invited back in 1925 to complete the event and win the cup. Those who competed for the first time in 1924 would take part in 1925 and 1926 for the cup, and so on. The accent was very much upon reliability, even longevity, but the ACO soon realized that the public cared very little for the niceties of the rules, and were much more interested in who actually won the race. In 1928 therefore Le Mans hosted the event named 'Les Vingt-Quatres Heures du Mans' for the first time, sub-titled 'Le Grand Prix de Vitesse et Endurance'.

Between 1923 and 1928 the full 17.4 km (10.8 mile) course was used, the sandy and stony surface bound but not treated with tar for the first two years. The cars and their drivers were ravaged by flying stones, which the competitors accepted as a natural hazard, but Durand was a strong campaigner for bitumen cladding, and by 1928 the entire circuit was properly sealed. In 1929 a link road was used to cut off the Pontlieue hairpin, where accidents were common, and in 1932 the ACO paid for, and retained exclusive use of a new link road sweeping from beyond the pits area to the right, now known as the Dunlop Curve, incorporating the Esses and joining the Le Mans-Tours highway at Tertre Rouge. Now the circuit was reduced in length to 13.45 km (8.35 miles) and remained thus until 1974 when a new section of road, referred to as the Porsche Curves, by-passed the notorious White House corner and slowed the cars substantially before they arrived in the area of the pits. Now, with the inclusion of a chicane loop before the Dunlop Bridge, the circuit length stands at 13.528 km.

Chapter 1

The 1920s

THERE has always been a tradition of sideshows at Le Mans, and the first edition on 26 and 27 May 1923 was a shining example. On Saturday evening a display of fireworks was held, depicting sporting scenes; wireless concerts were broadcast from the Eiffel Tower; a dance hall was opened in the outskirts of Le Mans; an American bar, a jazz band and an orchestra were all to be enjoyed. Moreover, promised the organizers, the grandstands and the pits (then, at Tertre Rouge) would be brilliantly lit, and army vehicles parked at the side of the route would provide extra illumination for the competitors. On Sunday a lunch was arranged for 500 people, but that was only of interest to members of the ACO. For the teams, 50 chickens, 150 gallons of hot soup and 450 bottles of champagne were provided!

Thirty–three cars started the inaugural event at four o'clock on the Saturday afternoon, representing 18 manufacturers. Of these, 16 were French and included four cars from Rolland-Pilain, three each from Lorraine-Dietrich and Chenard-Walcker, and two each from Berliet, Bignan, Voisin, Brasier, Corre La Licorne, Excelsior, Salmson and SARA. There was just one British entry, a 3 litre Bentley driven by John Duff and Frank Clement.

It was noted by *Autocar*'s correspondent, W. F. Bradley, that all the fastest cars save Bentley had braking for the front wheels, 'with which they gave marvellous exhibitions of their ability to stop quickly without skidding'. It was the lack of brakes, coupled with a dire fuel leak which once caused the Bentley to run out, that forced it down to fifth place overall.

The weather was dreadful for that first 24-hour race, with wind and rain throughout the night. The unsealed roads turned into a skating rink and clearly all-wheel braking was a great advantage (in

John Duff and Frank Clement were the first Britons to compete at Le Mans, driving their 3 litre Bentley to fifth place on distance in 1923 (BDC).

those early days some manufacturers, Bentley among them, believed that braking on the front wheels would cause uncontrollable skids, and the experience at Le Mans was instrumental in changing W. O. Bentley's mind). Neither Duff, a Canadian, nor Clement, a Bentley employee, wore headgear or goggles, but when conditions were at their best they did record the fastest lap of the race at 66.69 mph.

The race was 'won' — although official results were not declared, according to the Rudge-Whitworth rules — by André Lagache and René Leonard in a 3 litre Chenard-Walcker, who covered 2,209 km (1,372.9 miles) at an average speed of 92 km/h (57.2 mph).

The rules were fairly straightforward and were designed to encourage a variety of manufacturers. Cars up to 1,100 cc capacity need have only two seats, 60 kg (132 lb) of ballast was carried to represent a passenger, and the cars had to cover at least 920 km (571 miles) in 24 hours; all other cars had to have four seats installed, and would carry 180 kg (396 lb) of ballast to represent three passengers. Those up to 2,000 cc had to cover 1,200 km (745 miles), up to 3,000 cc 1,350 km (839 miles) and over that, 1,600 km (995 miles). A percentage of the total mandatory minimum had to be covered in each six-hour period, otherwise disqualification would follow.

Only the driver could work on the car, using tools and equipment which had to be carried in the vehicle, and at least 20 laps had to be completed before petrol, oil or water could be added. In 1924 a further rule was introduced, stipulating that open touring cars had to complete 20 laps with the hood raised!

More suitably equipped — with front wheel brakes, headgear and goggles! — Duff and Clement returned to Le Mans victoriously in 1924. After the race Duff (left) and Clement pose with the legendary W. O. Bentley (BDC).

In 1924 the 24-hour race was moved to 14-15 June in hope of better weather, and it was indeed sunny and warm. Although the number of starters went up to 40 there was still only one British entry, again a 3 litre Bentley in the hands of John Duff and Frank Clement, and despite some time-consuming difficulties they narrowly beat the only La Lorraine team survivor, by a margin of one lap.

The Bentley was improved in having four-wheel brakes, but the 2,996 cc four-cylinder engine developed no more than 80 bhp at 3,500 rpm despite having four valves per cylinder and twin spark plugs. With high gearing it would reach 90 mph (145 km/h) on the long straights and in the early stages of the race. The three-car La Lorraine team was overshadowed by the Chenard-Walckers (one of which made the fastest lap at an average speed of 111.17 km/h (69.08 mph)), and by the Aries and Bignan models.

All the leading French entries retired within eight hours, and the Bentley was handicapped by weak shock absorbers and by gear-changing difficulties. In the last hour, with victory in sight, the Bentley was further delayed by a swollen hub, and in fact its last five laps were disallowed for failing to reach the statutory minimum, producing a desperately close finish.

Even including the last five laps, the Bentley's distance was still 53 km (32.9 miles) short of the record established the year before, which says a lot for the performance of the Chenard-Walcker team, and it was one of the French company's smaller cars in the 1,100 cc class, driven by Glaszmann and de Zuniga, that captured the Rudge-Whitworth Cup in 1926.

Typical of the touring cars of its day was the 3 litre Diatto driven by Rubietti and Vesprini. This one failed to reach the minimum distance for classification (ACO).

Only 17 cars finished the race in 1924, rather than 30 (of 33) finishers in 1923, and the failure rate which was maintained in future years indicated that the cars were actually *racing*; for the first edition most competitors, fearful of what faced them, had toured the distance.

Two 3 litre Bentleys were entered for the 1925 race but neither lasted very long, failing to cover 20 laps without refuelling; Duff's car was able to continue, though how this happened wasn't clear to the organizers, but retired later when the carburettor flange split and caused a fire in the engine compartment. The Chenard-Walckers were again fast, Lagache's raising the lap record to 112 km/h (69.6 mph), but victory was taken at record speed by the 3.5 litre La Lorraine of Gérard de Courcelles/André Rossignol, covering a record distance of 2,334 km (1,450 miles). Another La Lorraine was third, and between them was the 3 litre Sunbeam driven by Jean Chassagne and S. C. H. 'Sammy' Davis which was still running despite having a cracked chassis.

There was only one consolation for Bentley in 1925, and that was the prize for being the quickest team away after the hoods had been raised! This was the first time the famous Le Mans start was seen, drivers running across the track to their cars when the signal was given at four o'clock, and just to make things more difficult those with convertible tops had to raise the hood before driving away.

An American car entered the French race in 1925, a Chrysler which finished in sixth place overall (another practised, but did not start). Now, only three years after its inception, the 24-Hours was becoming an important fixture, drawing competitors from many parts of the world as well as huge crowds of spectators. Whether the population flocks to the Sarthe to see the cars or just to have a good time has never been clear, but the ACO's policy of offering as many attractions as possible was clearly a good one.

In 1926 the Willys-Overland company sent three cars from America, two Overlands and a Willys-Knight. One Overland was wrecked during practice, and the sleeve-valve Willys-Knight dropped out on the seventh lap, but the remaining Overland ran well to seventh place overall.

The Bentleys, however, were not successful. W. O. Bentley's company had run into serious financial difficulties and was taken over by the South African diamond millionaire Woolf Barnato, who stepped up the challenge with a three-car team. This year the pits and the start had been moved from Tertre Rouge to their present placing midway between Arnage and the town of Le Mans.

A contemporary photograph of a Chenard et Walcker, the marque which won the inaugural race in 1923 and the coveted Coupe Triennial in 1925 (ACO).

The Bentleys, all still 3 litre models but now boasting around 90 horsepower, were among the leaders until Sunday morning, when one retired with a broken valve and another with broken rocker gear. The third, driven by Sammy Davis and Dr Dudley Benjafield, was

Right *A fine cornering shot of the Duller/Clement Bentley in 1926, emphasizing the greasy conditions the drivers had to cope with. The car retired with a broken valve (BDC).*

Below *W. O. Bentley and George Duller pictured before the race with 'Old Number 7', the car which survived a crash and went on to a famous victory driven by Dr 'Benjy' Benjafield and Sammy Davis (BDC).*

contesting second place when it ran out of brakes and out of road, at Mulsanne 20 minutes from the finish. Nevertheless it was classified sixth behind a trio of triumphant La Lorraine models and a pair of Italian 2 litre OMs.

The La Lorraine of Robert Bloch and André Rossignol was the first ever to exceed a 100 km/h (62 mph) average for the 24 hours — in fact all three entries did so — and Gérard de Courcelles, in the second-placed 3½ litre La Lorraine, also established a new course record in 9 min 3 sec, an average of 114.44 km/h (71.11 mph).

It was clear to Bentley that his cars were outpaced by the Lorraines, and of the three cars entered in 1927 two were 3 litre models, the third was the still experimental 4,398 cc version, still based on the same four-cylinder engine but with a much wider bore, of 100 mm, and a shorter stroke of 140 mm. The power, now, was up to 110 bhp, and Frank Clement was able to chop a huge 17 sec off the lap record early in the race.

Soon after darkness closed in, the entire Bentley team was the victim of a legendary accident, caused by a Schneider spinning and half blocking the road at the White House turn. Callingham's 4½ litre Bentley went into the ditch and rolled, followed moments later by Duller's 3-litre Bentley which was then two laps behind its more powerful team-mate. Sammy Davis, close behind, avoided the ditch but sustained extensive damage, the most serious being to the front dumb-iron which put out the front wheel alignment.

It took the Englishman half an hour to get going again, after replacing the wheel, rigging up a new headlamp, securing the battery box and strapping up the running board. Torrential rain made the proceedings a misery, and the sole 3 litre Aries of Laly/Chassagne seemed to have the race completely under control until the fuel pump began to fail, cutting its lead to one lap. Then, 90 minutes from the end, the Aries retired, handing a historic win to Davis and Benjafield all of 350 km (217 miles) ahead of a pair of 1.1 litre Salmsons.

Only 22 cars started the race in 1927, the world's economic slump combining with tougher regulations about refuelling to deter the leading French teams of La Lorraine and Chenard-Walcker, and of those only seven teams finished. Interesting entries were the two 1.5 litre, eight-cylinder SCAP cars, and the Tracta which was the first front-drive car ever to appear in a competition. Constructor Grégoire finished the race despite driving with a bandaged head!

Bentley had now won the race twice, but would go on to three further successes in 1928, 1929 and 1930. Remarkably Woolf Barnato, owner of the marque, would be the winner on each occasion, becoming the first man to record a hat-trick of victories, and the only man to have won on the three occasions he took part.

Neither, it seems, did he 'pull rank' and claim the best car; on the contrary, he left the running of the team entirely to Bentley, and if there was any difference between the cars he would tend to take the inferior one.

Right *The victorious Bentley number 3 rounds the Pontlieue hairpin, on the outskirts of Le Mans, ahead of Baron d'Erlanger's sister car which was badly damaged in the White House crash (driven by Duller) (Dunlop).*

Below *By 1928 most of the circuit had been paved, and this startline picture of the winning Bentley, driven by Woolf Barnato and Bernard Rubin, captures the atmosphere of the early races (BDC).*

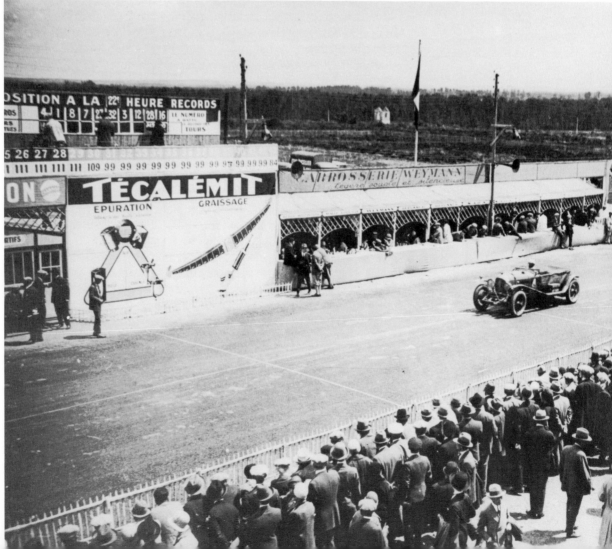

The victory in 1928 was also the hardest, faced with a 4.9 litre Stutz Black Hawk and four 4.1 litre Chryslers — the Americans were really out to make their name, and came near to succeeding. All three Bentleys were 4½ litre models, and initially they led the field, their aerodynamics improved by fitting fold-down windscreens since the hoods no longer needed to be erected at the start.

It was soon clear that the race of 1928 would be the finest yet, for although the Bentleys had speed enough to win, so too did the Stutz. Sir Henry (Tim) Birkin led from the start with Barnato and Clement following, but Brisson's Stutz was up there too, its straight-eight engine, which developed 125 bhp, and its hydraulic brakes enabling the French drivers to match every move made by the Bentley team. Just 20 laps into the race a rear tyre blew out at speed on Birkin's car, jammed the brakes, and caused the heavy car to slide into a ditch as it limped back to the pits. Birkin and his co-driver Jean Chassagne lost three hours altogether, but would set a new record on the last lap of the race, at 82.06 mph (132.05 km/h), and finish in fifth place.

The Bentleys of Clement and Barnato now led the Stutz, but on the twenty-sixth lap, soon after the first fuel stop, the Clement/ Benjafield car stopped in an oil haze caused by a fracture in the oil pipe serving the overhead camshaft. At half distance the car was back to third position, slowed by dawn mist, but then retired from the contest with a complete loss of water. The team kept the real reason a strict secret, for the chassis frame had cracked and dislodged the radiator, and this might well happen to the Barnato/Bernard Rubin car as well.

On Sunday morning the Stutz team had its own problem, the car jumping out of top gear in its three-speed transmission, and at midday Barnato's car was two laps clear at the head of the field; third, then, was the Chrysler of Stoffel and Rossignol, but that was nine laps behind.

In the last half-hour of the race the Bentley's slender lead was threatened when the chassis cracked, just as the team feared. Barnato slowed right down as his water temperature gauge went past the 100° mark, and the Stutz team increased its speed. On the Bentley's final lap the chassis broke altogether, jamming the throttle at 1,500 rpm (45 mph), and causing the door to swing open! 'It was just a question of keeping the thing together for one more lap,' said the owner, after taking the flag just 13 km (8 miles) ahead of the Stutz. His car had, all the same, shattered the distance record at 2,669.2 km (approximately 1,659 mile), and Birkin held a lap record that would never be broken, since the original Pontlieue hairpin was by-passed the following year.

Behind the Stutz were two of the Chryslers, hotly pursued by Birkin's Bentley. Then came the little 1.5 litre Alvis, which outlasted new cars from Aston Martin and Lagonda, and featured front-wheel drive like the Tracta team, which also finished intact.

The revised Pontlieue corner is taken at speed by the 6.6 litre Bentley of Barnato and Birkin, winning the race ahead of a trio of 4½ litre models (BDC).

Drivers had to refuel the cars unaided, and in 1929 Tim Birkin is seen using a collector box to speed the process. Despite the greater thirst of the 6½ litre car it finished 73 miles ahead of its team-mates (BDC).

By comparison, the 1929 race was a rout for Bentley, and a triumph for the new six-cylinder Speed Six version which led from start to finish in the hands of Barnato and Birkin, and behind it was a trio of 4.4 litre Bentleys driven by Kidston/Dunfee, Benjafield/d'Erlanger and Clement/Chassagne. The Stutz team (fifth) and Chrysler (sixth and seventh) were soundly beaten, while in eighth place came another British newcomer, the 1.5 litre Lea Francis.

With 180 bhp available, the drivers of the 6½ litre Bentley Speed Six were able to cruise along the straights comfortably at 100 mph (167 km/h), and after his first lap, at an average of 76 mph (122.3 km/h) from a standing start, Birkin passed the pits with not another car in sight, and by Sunday morning the Bentley was 70 miles (122

Only 18 cars started the 24-Hour race in 1930, nine of which finished, so the pits must have been fairly quiet during the hours of darkness (BDC).

km) ahead of its 4½ litre stable-mates, despite having been slowed down from 4 am.

Bentleys cleaned up with the top four positions, fifth was the only Stutz of three to start (driven by Bouriat and Philippe) and sixth was the Chrysler of Benoist and Stoffel. The Stutz team was in disarray, for the Brisson/Chiron entry caught fire while being refuelled, putting Brisson into hospital with burns; Louis Chiron tried to drive solo for the remaining 18 hours, but was thwarted by a holed fuel tank, and British record-breaker George Eyston, in another Stutz, retired for the same reason.

The presence of the awesome 7 litre, supercharged Mercedes SSK 38-250 in the 1930 Le Mans 24-Hours would keep the five-car Bentley team at full stretch for many hours. There was interest, too, in the latest Stutz powered by a 5.3 litre straight-eight engine boasting twin overhead camshafts and 32 valves, though the power was far less than it should have been at 160 bhp. The Mercedes, driven by Rudi Caracciola and Christian Werner, developed a prodigious 225 bhp, but the Roots supercharger had to be used with caution — the drivers were told never to push the throttle to the floor in first gear, nor at very low or very high speeds, and then only for 15 seconds at a time! It would, therefore, enable the car to reach its top speed of 120 mph (193 km/h) very quickly, but would not be used for more than a fraction of the time.

The Bentley team took three 6½ litre models to Le Mans. Work on the cylinder heads by Harry Weslake had raised the power from 160 bhp to about 190 bhp, and they were backed by a pair of new supercharged 4½ litre cars backed by the Hon Dorothy Paget, each one developing a stated 170 bhp at the rear wheels which indicated more than 200 bhp at the flywheel.

Able to spin the Mercedes' rear wheels in any gear, Caracciola led the Bentleys for four laps, and a daring passing manoeuvre at Mulsanne Corner by Birkin, in a 'blower' Bentley, resulted in a buckled rear mudguard for the Englishman, followed by a pit stop to pull the metal away from the tyre.

Above *The focal point of the 1930 event was the presence of the magnificent 7.1 litre Mercedes SS driven by Rudolf Caracciola and Christian Werner (pictured). The German car and its five Bentley adversaries were evenly matched for ten hours, until the Mercedes' battery failed and led to retirement (BDC).*

Right *Woolf Barnato (right) became the first Le Mans competitor to achieve a 'hat trick' of victories, seen here after the 1930 race with Glen Kidston (BDC).*

Bentley's fourth successive Le Mans victory was achieved in 1930 without Jack Dunfee's 'Speed Six', shared with Sammy Davis, which became lodged in the sand at Pontlieue (BDC).

The white German car led the race for hour after hour, while the supercharged Bentleys devoured their tyres and could offer no sort of threat, eventually retiring on Sunday morning with valve and piston failures. Dunfee planted his Speed Six Bentley in the sandbank at Mulsanne, and the Mercedes' real challenge came from *patron* Barnato with Glen Kidston as his co-driver. Driving the same car as Barnato had driven to victory in '29, they led by three minutes, less than half a lap, at midnight but they had to stop for an unscheduled tyre change, and again the Mercedes took the lead.

At 2.30 am, the Mercedes, announced by the scream of its supercharger as it sped round the track, slowed and was driven to the pits with dimmed lights. The battery had given out, and since the Germans were not allowed to fit a spare dynamo they had to retire from the contest. As a tribute to the car, clerk-of-the-course Charles Faroux allowed it to remain on the pit apron for the remainder of the race, rather than be banished to the 'cemetery'.

Both the Stutz entries had retired, the 1.8 litre supercharged Alfa Romeo was not fast enough to threaten the leaders, and the two Speed Six Bentleys now controlled the race from a pair of 2.3 litre Talbots, British cars with engines designed by George Roesch. In the smaller class the 1.5 litre Lea Francis was again a winner, in sixth place overall, beating the newcomer Bugatti team from Molsheim.

Woolf Barnato became a three-times winner at Le Mans, and led the Derby company's sixth success in the 24-hour race. Sadly, this was to be Bentley's last official appearance, for in the wake of the Wall Street crash and world recession the company was in dire financial difficulties. Bentley's reputation was never higher, but the products offered for sale could find few customers.

Chapter 2

The 1930s

E TTORE Bugatti had called the Bentleys 'the fastest lorries in the world', but the compliment rebounded on him in 1931! There were no 'factory' Bentleys in the race (one privately–owned car retired early), and although the Derby cars had been big and heavy, they had been durable. The Bugatti brothers, Ettore and Jean, entered a three-car team for the race in 1931. The touring bodies were painted black, and it was claimed that the type 50s' 4.9 litre eight-cylinder engines produced 275 horsepower. At close on two

tons apiece, though, they were almost as heavy as the Bentleys, and tyre strength would prove to be a major problem.

The era of heavy, big-engined cars was over, for the time being. The cars to look at were the new, scarlet Alfa Romeo type 8C 2300 supercharged models, with eight cylinders and 2.3 litres. Even with four-seater bodies they weighed less than 1,000 kg (2,200 lb), light by today's standards, developed 153 horsepower and had a top speed of 110 mph (177 km/h).

Former 'Bentley boys' Earl Howe and Tim Birkin drove one of the new Alfas, under pressure in the early stages by the Bugattis and by a 7.1 litre Mercedes, privately entered this time by Ivanowski and Stoffel. The German car led handsomely for the first hour, but was then slowed as the team was seriously concerned about tyre life, and the Louis Chiron/Achille Varzi Bugatti was also slowed as it threw tyre treads.

After two-and-a-half hours of racing the unfortunate Maurice Rost had a tread thrown from his Bugatti at Hunaudières, the fastest part of the long straight. It wrapped itself round a brake drum, putting him violently off the road and into an enclosure where one spectator was killed and several more hurt. Rost, too, was badly injured, and as the other Bugattis were having similar problems the team was withdrawn.

A new breed of car heralded the 1930s, the Alfa Romeo 8C 2300 taking four consecutive victories. Bentley had withdrawn and in the absence of the large capacity green cars Earl Howe and Tim Birkin switched to the Italian make to record a fine success in 1931 (Alfa Romeo).

A change of equipment, from Engelbert to Dunlop, kept the Mercedes SSK in contention but Howe and Birkin established a clear lead which they kept to the end, although their sister-car retired off the road after the transmission locked up. The Howe/Birkin Alfa Romeo was the first ever to exceed 3,000 km (1,864 miles) in 24 hours, their 3,017 km (1,875 miles) being 112 km (69.6 miles) more than the second-placed Mercedes managed. Third were the double-barrelled British drivers, Saunders-Davies and Rose-Richards, whose 3 litre Talbot covered 2,837 km (1,763 miles). A new name in the list of finishers was that of Aston Martin, a 1.5 litre model finishing fifth behind a La Lorraine, while the only other machine to finish was the 1.1 litre Caban.

This was the start of a new era, and Alfa Romeo would continue to dominate the race in 1932, 1933 and in 1934. As the Italian make was gaining ascendancy in Grand Prix racing, so there seemed to be no effective challenge from Bugatti, Mercedes or even the British Talbot make which seemed to make a habit of finishing third, well outdistanced.

The race in 1932 was significant in that the organizing committee had built a new section of road from the pits area to Tertre Rouge, bypassing the outskirts of Le Mans completely, and incorporating the famous 'Esses' at its halfway point. The length of each lap was reduced from 16.34 km (approximately 10.15 miles) to 13.492 km (8.385 miles) and the plan of the course was now established for almost half a century, though modifications between the White House and the pits would make the course safer in the 1970s. The course

Luigi Chinetti (facing the camera) recorded his first Le Mans success in 1932 with an Alfa Romeo shared with Raymond Sommer. He would win again in 1934 . . . and again in 1949, driving a Ferrari, though by then he was an American national (ACO).

was also marginally slower, though Alfa Romeo's development would soon push the averages upwards.

No fewer than six Alfa Romeos took part in the 1932 event, faced by two Bugatti type 55s in the 25-car field. Only three cars had capacities greater than 3 litres and they all crashed early in the race, a privately–entered Bentley being the first to do so at the White House on the opening lap. Two hours later after setting a new lap record Minoia's Alfa Romeo hit the parked Bentley and was soon joined by the Stutz and Marinoni's privately–entered Alfa, making another scene of carnage like that in 1927.

The battle between the Alfas of Howe/Birkin and Raymond

Celebrating after their success in 1932 are Luigi Chinetti and Raymond Sommer. Between them is M. A. Martin, Prefect of the Sarthe province (ACO).

Approaching the pits at speed is the 1932 winner, the Alfa Romeo 8C of Chinetti and Sommer. Compared with the Bentleys the Italian car was substantially lower, smaller, lighter and wider-tyred (Alfa Romeo).

Sommer/Luigi Chinetti lasted almost until half distance, when the British crew retired with a head gasket failure. Sommer's car had an exhaust manifold split so badly that Chinetti (then of Italian nationality) became quite ill, but Sommer seemed to be immune and drove for 21 hours to take victory. Second, only two laps behind, were the Italians Cortese and Guidotti in another Alfa Romeo and third (a massive 500 km (310 miles) behind!) were Brian Lewis and Tim Rose-Richards in their Talbot. The Bugattis, alas, failed to finish though they gave good account of themselves, one quitting second place with a blown piston and the other retiring from third position at noon.

Alfa Romeo was in such financial difficulties that it had to be nationalized in 1933, and would remain in the hands of the state until bailed out by the Fiat Group in 1987. Its racing department was officially closed, but factory-supplied cars would continue to appear with administration by the new Scuderia Ferrari, which organized the most convincing success yet.

Five Alfa Romeos took part, two of them short-wheelbase 'Mille Miglia' examples, and this time Raymond Sommer was joined by the Italian ace Tazio Nuvolari. Luigi Chinetti had a French co-driver, Varent, while Lewis and Rose-Richards forsook their Talbot to join the ranks of Alfa Romeo customers. The early stages of the race were made entertaining by the Duesenberg entered by Prince Paul of Rumania, a 6.8 litre V8 powered American car developing some 250 horsepower. Its consumption was high, and it was disqualified after 22 laps for refuelling sooner than allowed.

There was really no opposition at all since the Bugatti brothers had given up for the time being, but the Alfa Romeos provided the best contest yet seen. In the Mille Miglia models Nuvolari and Sommer drove near the limit to battle with Chiron and Cortese; Nuvolari's car

VOITURE GAGNANTE Coupe Annuelle

VOITURE GAGNANTE de la Coupe Biennale

The incomparable Tazio Nuvolari (with goggles) surprisingly only won at Le Mans once, in 1933, sharing victory with Sommer (beret). Nuvolari drove sensationally in the closing stages to overtake Chinetti on the last lap, and beat him by 400 metres! (Alfa Romeo).

lost time with a leaking fuel tank . . . which was patched with chewing gum. At three-quarter distance Cortese rolled his Alfa out of the contest at the Esses, but Chinetti and Varent kept up the pressure to the end.

The last lap saw Nuvolari at his best, challenging Chinetti, and the lead changed hands three times in the final 13 km (8 miles). Chinetti missed a gear at Arnage and Nuvolari took the race by ten seconds after breaking the lap record no fewer than nine times . . . but the fastest lap of the race, a new record, went to Sommer in 5 min 31.4 sec, an average of 146.386 km/h (90.97 mph). It was, in fact, a full ten seconds faster than Minoia's record of the previous year, in a similar car.

British cars did rather well, a 1.1 litre Riley finishing fourth, 1.5 litre Aston Martins fifth and seventh, and a new 750 cc MG finishing sixth. They were quick for their size and reliable too, but to keep things in perspective, the Riley of Peacock and van der Becke was 462 km (287 miles) behind the third-placed Alfa Romeo of Lewis and Rose-Richards.

Encouraged by their successes, Aston Martin and Riley entered full works teams for the race in 1934 ranged, hopelessly it seemed, against four privately–entered Alfa Romeos — still the magnificent, supercharged 8C 2300 models — various Bugattis, and a pair of

Alfa's fourth and last victory was in 1934 when Chinetti avenged his narrow defeat assisted by Philippe Etancelin. Their main opposition dissolved and they were followed home by seven small-capacity British cars, four Rileys, an MG and two Singers (Alfa Romeo).

Derby models with 2 litre V8 engines.

The Italian cars should have commanded the race, but they had their share of problems. Raymond Sommer's car burst into flames at Arnage after 14 laps, the Saunders/Clifford entry retired, and the cars of Howe/Rose-Richards and Chinetti/Etancelin duelled for the lead well into the night. The British crew held the advantage until their car lost an hour in the pits with electrical lighting problems, and retired at dawn with a broken clutch.

Chinetti and Etancelin had difficulties, too, with a leaking fuel tank which needed patching with chewing gum, but there was no pressure on them as all the faster competitors had fallen out, and they won at the slowest average speed for five years. Second and third were 1.5 litre Rileys and following up were three 1,100 cc cars, an MG and two more Rileys.

Four successive victories for the Alfa Romeo had turned this into a classic machine, and four of them were entered again for the 24-hour race of 1935. Their competition came from a pair of Lagondas, one with a Meadows straight-six engine tuned to 150 horsepower, the other with an older 2.3 litre four-cylinder motor, a pair of 3.2 litre Delahayes, French Talbots entered by company backer Antonio Lago, privately-entered Bugattis, two new Frazer Nashes, six Rileys and seven Aston Martins! In fact 36 of the 58 starters were British,

Right *By 1935 the main grand-stand was a substantial, two-tiered wooden building and spectators were safely separated from the track by fences and an earth embankment between. This is the second placed Alfa Romeo of Dreyfus and Stoffel, beaten by a single lap (Alfa Romeo).*

Below *A surprising winner in 1935 was the Fox and Nichol entered Lagonda 4.5 driven by John Hindmarsh and Louis Fontés. All four fancied Alfas gave trouble in the predominantly wet race and the Lagonda's Meadows straight-six engine was, perhaps, easier to drive (ACO).*

and so were 22 of the 28 finishers.

In summary, the 1935 race was wet virtually from start to finish, and the Alfa Romeos proved none too reliable. The 4.5 litre Lagonda driven by John Hindmarsh and Louis Fontés was on the Alfa Romeos' pace from the beginning, probably more flexible and easier to drive on the wet track, and was well placed to move into the lead as the Italian cars met problems.

Raymond Sommer, after leading by two laps, lost seven laps with electrical trouble early in the night but would retire later, the Chinetti/Gaston Alfa had two off-course adventures and retired, Earl Howe's car broke a piston, and that left just one Alfa driven by René-Louis Dreyfus and the lesser known Stoffel. They had lost time having the shock absorbers changed, but were catching the Lagonda rapidly in the last hour when Fontés made several stops with fading oil pressure.

At the very end Dreyfus reduced speed, believing that he had passed the stricken Lagonda . . . but his pits crew had made a serious mistake and the popular Frenchman was, in fact, the best part of a lap behind when the flag was shown! It was an unusual British victory, but well-deserved, and in third place was the 1.5 litre Aston Martin driven by Martin and Brackenbury, leading a 1.5 litre Riley.

The French had, it seemed, had enough of foreign domination and made a great effort for the 1936 race. The 60 entrants included not only Mercedes but Bugatti, Delage, Delahaye with eight cars, Lagonda, Simca, Citroën and a lot more besides, but the race had to be cancelled as a result of a national strike. It was a tragedy, for the ACO had spent a great deal of money on rebuilding the pits, modernizing the grandstands, improving the access roads and building a new rest centre for the drivers. All these features would be unused until 1937.

This was the era of Mercedes and Auto Union domination of Grand Prix racing, and now the French constructors gave sports cars and Le Mans their undivided attention, and would command the race for three years . . . until fighting the Germans became an obligation.

Of the 16 cars entered with engines larger than 3 litres, 14 were French and included a pair of aerodynamic 'Tank' Bugatti type 57s, seven 3.5 litre Delahayes, two Lago-Talbot 4 litre 'hemi-head' models and an interesting coupé version of the 3 litre Delage.

The two intruders in the big class, Sommer's Alfa Romeo and Hindmarsh's Lagonda, retired early, although the Alfa led the first five laps, and just within the first hour of the race a pile-up at the White House corner eliminated six cars, taking the lives of Pat Fairfield (Frazer Nash) and René Kippeurt (Bugatti).

Although the track was almost blocked the race continued, Jean-Pierre Wimille and Robert Benoist driving their 3.3 litre Bugatti like the wind and breaking the lap record repeatedly. The sister Bugatti driven by Veyron and Labric retired with a leaking fuel tank, making it impossible to cover the correct number of laps before refuelling, and when the Schell/Carrière Delahaye retired Wimille and Benoist found themselves with a lead of 16 laps, or an hour and a half in real terms.

Despite this great lead, which allowed them to slow from half distance, the Bugatti team smashed all the records, being the first to cover 2,000 miles (in fact, 3,287.9 km/2,043 miles) in the 24 hours. The Delahayes were second and third, the Delage fourth and Skeffington's 1.5 litre Aston Martin fifth, so the French could feel pretty pleased with the result.

Bugatti withdrew from the race in 1938, believing that a supercharged version of the type 57 'Tank' would be needed to deal with new 4.5 litre Delahaye and Talbot contenders . . . but the Molsheim concern had not yet completed its test programme. More than half the field of 42 cars was in French racing blue, led by a pair of Delahaye type 145 V12 models, developing over 200 bhp and derived from monoposto Grand Prix cars. Drivers included Pierre Dreyfus — the most popular man in France after beating the Mercedes team at Pau two months before — Louis Chiron, Comotti and Divo; behind them were five more 3.6 litre Delahayes, faced by a 4.5 litre Talbot straight-six for Luigi Chinetti and 'Fifi' Etancelin, five more 4 litre versions (two of them coupés), and a new coupé-bodied Alfa Romeo 8C 2900B, with supercharging, for Sommer and Biondetti.

As so often happens the new, pace-setting machines proved fragile and it was the less powerful models that came through to take the prizes. Comotti's Delahaye broke its gearbox within the first hour, and at the two-hour mark Dreyfus's Delahaye overheated badly and had to be withdrawn, its V12 engine ruined. After five hours the Etancelin/Chinetti Talbot retired with valve failure, leaving Raymond Sommer and his Italian co-driver to build upon a five-lap lead over the 3.6 litre Delahayes of Chaboud/Tremoulet and Serraud/Giraud-Cabantous.

Without any need to hurry the Alfa Romeo (or 'la rouge' as the French called it) built up a lead of 13 laps during the night, but just before midday the unthinkable happened and Biondetti brought the car to the pits with a broken valve. No-one was more surprised to win than Eugene Chaboud and Jean Tremoulet, for their Delahaye had lost all but top gear before midnight! The mechanics had prepared to wheel the car back to the paddock but Chaboud decided to carry on until the car would run no more . . . and behind them at the finish was another Delahaye which had developed a leak in the fuel tank even before the start.

Perhaps in 1939 the mood of the race was sombre, for the possibility of war with Germany seemed high. From Molsheim, close to the German border, came the Bugatti type 57 'Tank', now with Roots supercharging, 200 horsepower and a top speed of 150 mph. Jean-Pierre Wimille, winner in 1937, drove the car again accompanied by Pierre Veyron, chosen for his 'solid' (eg, reliable) perform-

The Bugatti type 57 recorded its second victory in June 1939, pictured before the start with drivers Jean-Pierre Wimille and Pierre Veyron. The 57C was prepared with Roots supercharging and 200 horsepower, and the 'tank' shape allowed it a top speed of 150 mph. Ten years before, the Bentleys barely reached 100 mph (ACO).

ances. The high quality field included two of the latest V12 engined Lagondas (designed by W. O. Bentley, but raced against his wishes), eight 3.6 litre Delahayes, three 4.5 litre Talbots and three more 4 litre versions, two 3 litre Delages, and the new coupé-bodied Alfa Romeo 6C 2500 for Raymond Sommer and ERA exponent Prince Birabongse (Bira) of Siam.

The Alfa Romeo was soon in trouble with plug and cylinder head problems, and would not last the evening, but the huge French crowd was enthralled by the battle between the Delage of Gérard and Monneret, the Delahaye of Mazaud and Mongin, and the Talbot of Chinetti and Mathieson.

After ten hours the quickest Delahaye caught fire and burned out, right in front of the pits, and Gérard's Delage gradually eased out a useful lead over Wimille's Bugatti which was being driven very cautiously, despite which it lost two laps due to a burst tyre. Mathieson visited the sand in the Talbot, and was forced to retire with a valve problem on Sunday morning, and then the Gérard/Monneret Delage slowed dramatically with a broken valve spring and lost 45 minutes in the pits.

Caution paid off for Wimille and Veyron who established a new distance record of 3,354.6 km (2,085 miles), at 139.781 km/h (86.87 mph), and finished five laps ahead of the Gérard/Monneret Delage. Third and fourth were the two 4.5 litre Lagonda V12s after a carefully planned race, and fifth was a 2 litre BMW 328.

There would not be another edition of 'Les Vingt-Quatre Heures du Mans' until 1949. Three months later Europe was at war, and in 1940 the Sarthe region was over-run by the German army, which would remain in occupation for four years . . .

Chapter 3

Starting again

D URING the war, the circuit area was badly damaged and required
an immense amount of money and time to restore. The British
army had made camp there in 1940, destroying the pits and
grandstands, and later the Germans cleared the area of trees to make
way for a prison camp. Even when the first post-war race was held in
June 1949, there were forbidden areas about which it was best not to
argue with the gendarmes, since they contained uncleared mines!

There were new pits and grandstands, though, and a quarter of a
million spectators paid their money to watch the resumed classic
race. Most of them were French, of course, but there were also
many British and American servicemen, and a number of the
Americans were over from the homeland, people like Briggs Cunningham and members of the recently-formed Sports Car Club of
America. Prominent, too, was Luigi Chinetti, twice a winner for Alfa
Romeo in the 1930s, but since 1946 a naturalized American who
would now import and race Ferraris.

With the passing of a wasted decade many things had changed. In
1949, not many manufacturers were yet in production with new
designs so the Automobile Club de l'Ouest decided to allow 'prototypes' to take part — cars which were intended for production but
which had not yet been offered for sale — and could not have known
what sort of Pandora's Box they had opened.

The cars were smaller, lighter, more powerful, and would soon be
a great deal faster than those of the 1930s. Until then, coupé bodies
and enclosed wheels had been rare objects of curiosity but now they
became a good deal more fashionable; aircraft design had shown the
importance of enclosing the wheels, for instance, and the smaller-
engined cars in particular had surprisingly good aerodynamics.

Except for the second edition, in 1950, the old names were swept

New name, old face. Ferrari's first appearance at the Sarthe in 1949 brought success, the 2 litre 166 MM model being driven by Lord Selsdon and third-time winner Luigi Chinetti (ACO).

aside, and a French make would not win the 24-hour race again until 1972. There were the new names of Ferrari, Jaguar, Cunningham, Allard, and Healey; Mercedes would return in 1952, and Professor Porsche preceded them by a year with aluminium-bodied type 356 sports cars — their successors would one day dominate the results totally. Aston Martin would make serious bids for victory, Ford of America would become a powerful force, and so, to, would Renault.

Ferrari was the first post-war winner, with the Tipo 166 powered by the Gioacchini Colombo-designed V12 engine. Although the engine capacity was only 2 litres, at 140 bhp the power was excellent, and examples were entered for Chinetti and Lord Selsdon, and for French drivers Dreyfus and Lucas.

The quality of the fuel supplied by the organizers was very poor indeed, a ternary mixture of petrol, benzole and ethanol, and was blamed for numerous engine failures. At first the powerful pre-war French cars made the running. The Delahaye of Chaboud and Pozzi led by two clear laps at the three-hour mark, but then it caught fire and was out of the race. Three Talbots, seven Delahayes and four Delages had seemed enough to ensure a French victory, but Chinetti's Ferrari was forever snapping at their heels (and the Italian-American stayed at the wheel for 22 hours, allowing his British co-driver Lord Selsdon just two hours in the night). Mairesse and Vallée led after six hours in their Talbot, but slipped back and retired after midnight with a broken connecting rod, by which time Chinetti was in the lead for good. Chasing in their 3 litre Delage were Louveau and Jover, who smelled victory in the last hour when Chinetti slowed with oil pouring from his clutch. The Ferrari kept going, slower and slower, to take victory by a single lap, while third place was claimed by H. J. 'Aldy' Aldington and British motor cycle

The Talbot Lago driven by Louis Rosier and his son, Jean-Louis, was a famous winner in 1950. The French were not to know it, but a blue car would not win again until 1972 (ACO).

champion Norman Culpan in a Frazer Nash 2 litre. Delage and Delahaye were fourth and fifth, while in sixth place was the magnificent pre-war Bentley 4.4 litre Corniche owned by Mr H. S. F. Hay, who interrupted his touring holiday with his family to take part in the race with Tommy Wisdom. Once the race was finished Mr Hay continued his tour, lacking only the overdrive!

The 1950 edition was the last to be won by a production line car, and in fact the 4.5 litre Talbot Lagos finished in first and second places, ahead of the 5.4 litre, Cadillac–engined Allard. Sixty entries

was an all-time record for the race and they included three Jaguar XK120s, with aluminium bodies but in virtually standard trim and five Ferraris including two with 2.3 litre V12 engines. There were also two Aston Martins owned by industrialist David Brown and powered by 2.5 litre, six cylinder engines taken from Lagonda, which make had been absorbed into the organization. From America, oil millionaire Briggs Cunningham had brought two Cadillacs, one a saloon and the other a slab-sided, open car dubbed 'Le Monstre', and they finished in tenth and eleventh places.

Feeling tired? 1950 race winner Louis Rosier drove for more than 23 hours, and changed a rocker shaft at 5 am. His son Jean-Louis, with duster, drove only two laps while papa ate a couple of bananas! On their right, in the trilby hat, is M. Vincent Auriol, President of the Republic (ACO).

Raymond Sommer had postponed his retirement to take part in the race. He was quickest in practice and led the first two hours of the race in his Ferrari 195S, but then a broken alternator mounting delayed him, and eventually caused him to withdraw. Chinetti's Ferrari lasted longer, lying third as darkness closed in, but retired with a broken axle joining the three 2 litre Italian cars in the paddock.

Louis Rosier and his son, Jean-Louis, fairly commanded the race throughout in their Talbot Lago although the sister car driven by Guy Mairesse and P. Meyrat was always close at hand, and led for a while when the Rosier entry had a setback. A five o'clock in the morning the engine rattled and the driver, Louis, had to spend 41 minutes changing a valve rocker shaft. Having done that he allowed his son to drive for two laps, while he ate a bunch of bananas, then carried on to the finish.

In the results the Rosiers beat Mairesse and Meyrat by three laps, with Sidney Allard and Tom Cole third in the Allard J2. Fourth was Donald Healey's 3.8 litre, Nash–engined Healey driven by Duncan Hamilton and Tony Rolt, then came two of the Aston Martin DB2s managed by John Wyer. Two little-known Argentinians, Juan-Manuel Fangio and Froilan Gonzalez, had driven a 3 litre, supercharged Simca Gordini but it never ran higher than ninth, and retired in the night with electrical problems. As for the Jaguars, they were short of brakes and two finished in twelfth and fifteenth places, but Bert Hadley and Leslie Johnson had been as high as second overall during the night and retired with engine problems shortly before the finish.

Chapter 4

The 1950s: a golden era

IN RETROSPECT the 1950s was the golden era at Le Mans with new, streamlined cars from Jaguar, Ferrari, Mercedes-Benz, Maserati, Aston Martin, Allard, Cunningham, Lancia, Nash Healey and Talbot Lago all battling for outright victories. Behind them, and very close sometimes, were new streamlined models in lower classes from Porsche, Bristol, Lotus, AC and Cooper, while in the 'baby class' for 750 cc models the DB, Monopole and Dyna Panhards regularly battled against the Renault 4 CVs. In 1954, for instance, the 745 cc DB Panhard of Bonné and Bayol covered 2,080 miles (3,346.7 km) in 24 hours, despite partly wet conditions, and if the clock could be turned back, would easily have won the race in 1949!

The Talbot Lago that won in 1950 was a thinly-disguised Grand Prix car with two seats and cycle-type mudguards, but in 1951 a new breed of sports racing car, the Jaguar C-type, heralded another era. The Coventry company, having seen all the possibilities opened up by the XK120 road cars the year before, prepared four space frame XK120 C-types, with beautifully sleek, aerodynamic body shapes evolved mathematically by Malcolm Sayer. All were powered by Jaguar's 3,441 cc straight-six engine, which developed 200 horse-power, with twin SU carburettors, and had maximum speeds approaching 160 mph (257 km/h) on the Mulsanne Straight.

The fastest of the Jaguars were driven by Stirling Moss with Jack Fairman and Peter Walker with Peter Whitehead, and their opposition came from many quarters. There were nine Ferraris, with a driver team including Luigi Chinetti and Louis Chiron; six Lago Talbots with Fangio and Gonzalez in the team; two Allard J2s, three Cunninghams, Rolt and Hamilton in a Nash Healey 3.8, and five Aston Martin DB2s with 2.6 litre engines.

Prospects for this epic race were wonderful, and millions of British

Right *Peter Whitehead ran the first Jaguar at Le Mans in 1950. He and John Marshall were as high as sixth overall before the brakes faded, and were classified fifteenth (A. Whyte).*

Below *The start in 1951, and Peter Walker's C-type is already leading two Cunninghams, a Talbot, and an Aston Martin (A. Whyte).*

Peter Whitehead takes the chequered flag in 1951, the Jaguar C-type's first race (A. Whyte).

enthusiasts kept their radio sets on throughout the 24 hours to keep up with the happenings in France. The weather was the only thing that spoiled the atmosphere, often wet and with a thunderstorm during the night.

Moss and Fairman were to be the 'hares', their job being to extend and break the Talbots, which they did very effectively. Leading right from the start, Moss's Jaguar was a lap ahead of the Walker/ Whitehead Jaguar at midnight with Gonzalez and Marimon two laps behind, Fangio and Rosier five laps behind. The Ferraris were disappointing as regards speed and reliability, while the Aston Martins were not really fast enough, although all five finished.

In the early hours Moss's Jaguar retired with a blown head gasket, Gonzalez's Talbot with a broken water system and Fangio's also with a cooling failure, and the misty dawn saw Walker and Whitehead firmly in the lead eight laps ahead of the Cunningham driven by Phil Walters and John Fitch. Fifth, then, was the Talbot driven by Mairesse and Meyrat, but this was trouble-free to the end and was classified second, ten laps behind the Jaguar. Third were Lance Macklin and Eric Thompson in their Aston Martin, the Feltham concern also claiming fifth, seventh, tenth and thirteenth places, while the best that Ferrari could manage was eighth with the 4.1 litre 'America' model driven by Chinetti and Lucas.

In twentieth place was an aluminium–bodied Porsche 356 entered by the factory — the first German car to be entered in a French sporting event since the war — and driven by the importer 'Toto' Veuillet and Edmond Mouche. They won the 1,100 cc class, too, in what was virtually a standard 356 with faired-in wheels, and could have had no idea that they had written the first lines in a whole chapter of Le Mans history.

Relaxing after their success are Peter Whitehead, Peter Walker in the car, and mechanic Joe Sutton (A. Whyte).

Production cars still had a place in the 24–hour race and throughout the 1950s Austin-Healeys, MGBs, Triumph TRs, Sprites and Midgets, ACs, Jowetts and Bristols were competing regularly, the manufacturers benefitting from enormous prestige and advertising potential. Jaguar and Aston Martin, though, raised the stakes greatly by preparing ever more powerful cars capable of winning, though their links with production models were still very strong.

Jaguar returned with three C-types in 1952, but the effort was self-defeating. In the weeks before the race the team had been persuaded that more speed would be needed on the Mulsanne Straight, and the front bodywork was restyled with smaller apertures to the radiators. There were signs of overheating during practice, in the cool of the evening, but it was too late to carry out any effective modifications and all three cars retired within three hours, all as a result of overheating.

The Ferraris were hardly in a better state, six of them retiring with assorted clutch, transmission and electrical problems although one of them, a type 340 'America' driven by Simon and Vincent, salvaged fifth place.

Mercedes had entered three 300 SL sports coupés based on their new 3 litre catalogue model, the straight-six engines developing 175 bhp. They seemed to be somewhat underpowered, in fact, and made very steady starts running ninth, tenth and eleventh at the end of the first hour. Their opposition did not come from Jaguar and Ferrari after all, but from the rapid 2.3 litre Gordini driven by Behra and Manzon, and from the 4.5 litre Talbot Lago driven single-handedly by Pierre Bouillon, also known as Pierre Levegh.

Karl Kling's Mercedes retired before midnight with its dynamo broken, and Behra's Gordini went out at half distance with seized brakes. Without respite Levegh ploughed on in the lead, four laps ahead of the two Mercedes at midday on Sunday, although it was noted that his driving was becoming increasingly ragged, and the Talbot was often four wheels off the track. It is hard to imagine, now, the strain of driving 2,330 miles (3,750 km) without once getting out of the car, but that is what the Frenchman did . . . bravely or foolishly, according to your loyalty. With just one hour to run Levegh

New shapes at Le Mans in 1952 were those of the Mercedes-Benz 300 SL Coupés, with gullwing doors that favoured the run-and-jump start (Daimler-Benz).

Left *The Mercedes of Hermann Lang and Fritz Reiss shattered the distance record, as did the second placed Mercedes of Helfrich and Niedermayer a lap behind at the finish* (Daimler-Benz).

selected first gear in the pre-selector gearbox when he meant to take third, and a connecting rod in the Talbot's engine snapped.

Mercedes swept on to their 1-2 finish, Hermann Lang and Fritz Reiss taking the honours, and although the three-pointed star would be represented again, this was Mercedes's single success at the Sarthe.

Jaguar made no mistakes at all in 1953, preparing three works C-types, and one for the Belgian Ecurie Francorchamps . . . and they finished first, second, fourth and ninth, with Walters and Fitch third in the Cunningham C-5R. This time the Ferraris, the supercharged Lancias and the Alfa Romeo Disco Volantes were truly put to flight, and the triumphant Jaguar team returned to a civic reception in Coventry.

The works Jaguars were similar to those which won in 1951, but the 3.4 litre engines were more powerful with 220 bhp, and for the first time they had a new disc brake system developed by Dunlop, an innovative feature which gave them an overwhelming advantage at the Mulsanne Corner on each lap. Peter Walker and Stirling Moss were in one car, Peter Whitehead and Jimmy Stewart in the second, and third, initially as reserves, were Tony Rolt and Duncan Hamilton.

It is part of Jaguar's folklore that Rolt and Hamilton were not guaranteed a race if all 60 invited teams took the start, and the two colourful Englishmen were, in fact, told on Friday evening that they would not be taking part. They drowned their sorrows in some style, but team manager 'Lofty' England found them in the early hours, sitting on a pavement, and told them that one team had withdrawn. They would start.

On Saturday afternoon they were far from well and tossed a coin

Right *Ferrari made a determined effort to win in 1953 with the 4½ litre 375 MM driven by Ascari and Villoresi. They duelled hard with the victorious Jaguar until the clutch failed on Sunday morning* (Autosport).

Right *All three Jaguars retired early in 1952 as a new nose profile, designed to raise the maximum speed, led to over-heating. Ian Stewart's Jaguar leads Duntov's Allard and Heldé's Ferrari at Tertre Rouge (A. Whyte).*

Below *Disc brakes helped Jaguar to their second 24-hour success in 1953, Duncan Hamilton followed here by the Ecurie National Belge Jaguar of Laurent/de Tornaco (A. Whyte).*

not to take the start. The fresh air soon cleared their hangovers, and after an hour the order was Moss (Jaguar), Villoresi (Ferrari), Rolt (Jaguar), Cole (Ferrari), then the Alfa Romeos of Kling and Fangio.

Moss made two stops in the second hour to have a blocked fuel pipe cleared, dropping to twenty-first place, and Villoresi took the lead, only to be passed by Rolt. The pace was extraordinary, Rolt setting a new lap record at 4 min 30 sec (115 mph (185 km/h)), more than 10 seconds quicker than Ascari had gone a year before in a Ferrari. Soon, though, Ascari recaptured the record at 4 min 27.4 sec (116.87 mph (188.12 km/h)), and would duel with Rolt and Hamilton throughout the night, until his clutch failed on Sunday morning.

One by one the challengers fell away. The Lancias were unexpectedly slow, and retired on Sunday. The 3 litre Aston Martin DB3S sports cars were no match for the Jaguars either and in the latter stages the only car that the Coventry team neded to worry about was the big Cunningham, which thundered on to third place. Whitehead and Stewart had run strictly to orders, and were fourth, a lap behind the Cunningham, at the finish.

A civic reception awaited the Jaguar team at the Coventry Town Hall in 1953 after the C-types finished first, second and fourth (A. Whyte).

What was remarkable about the race was its sheer speed, for the first seven cars to finish all exceeded 2,400 miles (3,861 km) for an average of over 100 mph (162 km/h). The Mercedes that had won

the year before would have been placed only ninth, though admittedly that race was partly wet, and the deeply-fatigued Rolt and Hamilton covered 2,540 miles (4,087 km).

There were no Mercedes in the race, nor in 1954, but there was no let-up in the titanic duel between Jaguar and Ferrari. Both manufacturers prepared new cars for the race, Jaguar's being new monocoque-chassis D-types, perhaps the most beautiful sports cars that have ever graced the circuit. Their lines were streamlined and evocative, longitudinal fins behind the tail fairings giving them a most distinctive appearance, though straightline stability was actually the reason for their design. Again, Malcolm Sayer had produced a classic shape, and again three cars were prepared for the contest. Each was powered by the 3.4 litre straight-six now developing 255 bhp at 6,000 rpm, and the maximum speed was up to 170 mph (273 km/h). Many people were concerned, though, that the cars were passing the open, unprotected pits at 140 mph (225 km/h), a recipe for disaster one day . . .

Ferrari responded with the V12 375 'Plus' models, three brutal machines with 5 litre engines developing close on 350 bhp. Pinin Farina designed the spyder bodywork and the rear suspension was a de Dion design, more effective probably than Jaguar's old-fashioned live axle layout.

Briggs Cunningham took three of his white and blue cars to the Sarthe, two of them powered by 5½ litre Chrysler V8 engines, the third by a Ferrari V12. The latter was rather new and untested, and retired after dawn with a broken axle. Aston Martin took three DB3S models, none of which was particularly fast, all failing to finish; and Bristol took three special-bodied, aerodynamic '450' models powered by 2 litre, BMW–origined engines which finished in line claiming seventh, eighth and ninth positions.

On a dry track the Ferraris certainly had the edge on the Jaguars, and dominated the hourly charts on Saturday evening: Froilan Gonzalez and Maurice Trintignant led Umberto Maglioli and Paolo Marzotto, third were Louis Rosier and Robert Manzon, chased by Stirling Moss/Peter Walker, Ken Wharton and Peter Whitehead, and Rolt and Hamilton all in Jaguars. Early evening brought rain, and now Moss moved ahead of the thundering scarlet Ferraris to lead the race, but British hopes were subdued when all three D-types made unscheduled stops to have blocked fuel filters changed. Moss's car dropped right back in the evening with brake problems which would lead to retirement, then Wharton and Whitehead lost gears in the night and retired with transmission failure, at dawn. Maglioli's Ferrari retired just before midnight with a broken axle, though, and Rosier's broke its gearbox as the sun rose on Sunday morning. Then, Rolt and Hamilton were on their own, always within striking distance of the Gonzalez/Trintignant Ferrari.

An incident with a slower car delayed the Jaguar midway through Sunday morning, and on a drying track Gonzalez put two laps

A controversial pit stop: Duncan Hamilton stops in the closing stages of the 1954 race for a change of goggles. Trintignant and Gonzalez beat the Jaguar by 2.5 km (A. Whyte).

between himself and the D-type. But then, with less than two hours to go, rain set in again and both the leaders were suffering. The Ferrari stubbornly refused to fire up again after a routine stop, and the seven minutes that elapsed seemed like an eternity to the Italians, and to the Jaguar team; Rolt was almost in sight when the Ferrari's V12 restarted and Gonzalez black-lined his way up the track.

Rolt's goggles had steamed up though. He stopped to change them and was frantically waved out again. He stopped again on the next lap, unable to see properly, and this time he was replaced by Hamilton, who would take up the contest to the finish. The track was almost dry for the last 30 minutes, and Gonzalez was able to eke out a lead of 2.5 km (1.5 miles) before four o'clock, one of the narrowest margins separating rival makes.

The tragic race

In 1955 Les Vingt-Quatre Heures du Mans had the makings of a magnificent contest, a three-way duel between Jaguar, Ferrari and Mercedes, with Aston Martin, Porsche and Bristol playing strong supporting roles. Mercedes sent three 300SLR models, virtually two-seat versions of the Grand Prix 'streamliner', with controversial air flap brakes, and included Pierre Levegh in their team, although Fangio/Moss and Kling/Simon were clearly to be the pace-setters. Ferrari presented entirely new cars, the 121 LM model powered by

3,750 cc six-cylinder engines, while Jaguar further refined the D-types with 'big-valve' heads, and had Mike Hawthorn leading their team. Power outputs were 300 bhp for the Mercedes, 280 bhp for the Ferraris and 270 bhp for the Jaguars.

For two hours there was little to choose between the teams. Eugenio Castellotti led for Ferrari, but was passed in the second hour by Hawthorn's Jaguar and Fangio's Mercedes, the three rarely separated by more than a few seconds. Then, when the first refuelling stops were due, the worst accident in motor racing history occurred, a disaster that would take the lives of 83 spectators and that of Pierre Levegh.

Hawthorn was castigated in the aftermath, but careful analysis of the events exonerated him. At the 2½ hour mark he overtook Lance Macklin's Austin Healey after the White House, and correctly moved to the right-hand side of the road to slow down and enter the pits. Behind him, then, was Macklin, with Levegh (a lap behind) and Fangio (eight seconds behind) catching fast.

Macklin may not have been expecting Hawthorn to slow as he did, 400 m from the pits, and pulled round the back of the Jaguar rather sharply to the centre of the road. Levegh seemed not to have anticipated any of this and, at 140 mph (225 km/h), his Mercedes hit

The narrowness of the main straight, including the pits working area, is clearly seen in the start picture of Le Mans in 1955. It was a disastrous event, and the Mercedes team already looks cramped for space (Daimler-Benz).

the back of the Austin-Healey and flew into the air, crash-landing on to the concrete barrier and earthworks that should have protected the spectators. Levegh was thrown out and fatally injured, while the blazing magnesium engine scythed through the packed spectator enclosure.

It was the most awful accident imaginable. The ACO kept the race going, and kept news of the accident off the public address system in order to maintain calm and enable the rescue services to do their work. Hawthorn was sent on for another lap, and was almost overcome with grief and self-blame when he came out of the cockpit. Macklin was unhurt, but deeply shocked, while Fangio miraculously avoided the carnage and went on to lead the race for several more hours.

During the night the two remaining Daimler-Benz entries were withdrawn, on instructions from Stuttgart, and Mike Hawthorn and Ivor Bueb were able to lead the race from the Maserati 300S of Musso and Valenzano, which lasted considerably longer than most people expected, until midday on Sunday. Second, then, was the Aston Martin DB3S of Peter Collins and Paul Frère which finished three laps behind the D-type, and comfortably ahead of the Ecurie Francorchamps D-type.

The ill-fated Pierre Levegh runs wide to overtake a Salmson, in pursuit of Fangio at Mulsanne Corner. The Frenchman was killed shortly afterwards, tragically along with 83 spectators (Daimler-Benz).

All the Ferraris retired before half distance with assorted engine and transmission failures, and in fourth, fifth and sixth places were three Porsche type 550 sports cars, powerful 1.5 litre machines which ran monotonously for the 24 hours. So too did the Bristols, which remarkably occupied the same seventh, eighth and ninth positions that they claimed the year before.

Somehow motor racing had to survive the world-wide condemnation that followed the race. Although racing was banned in Switzerland from that time, the ACO decided, as expected, to keep the event in existence. The 1956 race, though, was delayed until the end of July in order to complete major revisions to the circuit, especially widening the track between the White House and the pits, including a braking zone entering the lane, and improving spectator protection. They could do no less, but still the pits were an open part of the track; indeed they needed to be since the traditional 'Le Mans start' was maintained, drivers running across the track to jump in and start the race.

Prototype cars with production lower than 50 were limited to a maximum capacity of 2,500 cc which rather took the wind out of Ferrari's and Maserati's sails, but Jaguar and Aston Martin had made enough D-types and DB3S models to qualify. The Cunningham team was disbanded, having tried gallantly for a number of years to win with American–constructed cars, and now there were no more Talbots or Mercedes to continue the battle.

Fuel tank sizes were restricted to 120 litres (26.4 gallons) and cars had to run for a minimum of 34 laps before refuelling. Full width windscreens were another imposition on design. The cars would be

Above *In 1955, the class winning 1.1 litre Porsche RS of Duntov and Veuillet chases the 1.1 litre Cooper Climax driven by Wadsworth and Brown* (Porsche)

Right *Architect of Jaguar's five victories, Lofty England, with Duncan Hamilton* (A. Whyte).

little slower, Jaguar's power being only slightly reduced to 263 bhp as Lucas fuel injection was fitted for the first time, to improve efficiency. Ferrari's hope was the 625 model which had a six-cylinder, 2.5 litre engine installed in the Testa Rossa chassis, but its top speed was restricted by the new windscreen regulation.

Jaguar entered three fuel-injected D-types supported by a single Ecurie Ecosse entry, driven by Ron Flockhart and Ninian Sanderson, and with another entered by Equipe National Belge for Jacques Swaters and Freddy Rousselle, it looked as though Jaguar would have little difficulty in dominating this race.

The best laid plans go awry, and within minutes of the start Jaguar's aspirations were dashed. It was drizzling at the start, the tarmac was treacherously slippery, and on his second lap Paul Frère locked-up his brakes approaching the Esses and slid into the barrier. Jack Fairman, in the third works car, was able to stop in time but was hit by the works Ferrari of the Marquis de Portago, all three cars being reduced to scrap. Then Hawthorn's Jaguar started misfiring badly, and it took some hours to trace the fault to a hairline crack in the fuel injection lines. Hawthorn and Bueb did not start motoring properly until the evening, when they were in fortieth place and 21 laps behind leaders Moss and Collins, in their Aston Martin DB3S.

For Ecurie Ecosse, Flockhart and Sanderson drew ahead of the Aston Martin, Moss and Collins feeling the lack of half a litre in engine capacity. When the Aston Martin lost second gear on Sunday morning it stood no chance of making up its deficit, losing valuable seconds in accelerating from Mulsanne Corner, and Britain's top sports car drivers did well to keep the margin to 10 km (6 miles) at the finish. Third were Maurice Trintignant and Olivier Gendebien in their Ferrari LM, followed by the Belgian D-type, a works Porsche 550 RS driven by Wolfgang von Trips and Richard von Frankenberg, then Hawthorn and Bueb in the surviving works Jaguar. Two 1,100 cc Coventry Climax–engined cars, a Lotus 11 and a Cooper, took seventh and eighth places.

In October of that year, 1956, the Jaguar factory announced its withdrawal from motor racing. It had achieved all that was possible, and demands on engineering and production were ever more urgent. The team's cars would be transferred on generous terms to Ecurie Ecosse, and the deal would include two of the new 3.8 litre engines which, with fuel injection, developed 297 bhp. Ferrari and Maserati, though, returned with more powerful cars as prototypes were again admitted; Ferrari's entries were the 412 models (4 litres, 12 cylinders) for Peter Collins/Phil Hill and Mike Hawthorn/Luigi Musso, and Maserati's were tipo 450 (4.5 litres) for Stirling Moss/Harry Schell and Jean Behra/André Simon.

Aston Martin's strength was growing, with new DBR1 models for Tony Brooks/Noel Cunningham-Reid and Roy Salvadori/Les Leston, but still the 3 litre engine was short of vital power.

Power was also the key to the first hours of the race as Collins and

Hawthorn in Ferraris duelled with the Maseratis of Moss and Behra. The Italian cars were soon exhausted, though. Collins's Ferrari retired in the second hour with engine failure, Behra's Maserati in the third hour with axle failure, Moss's Maserati in the fifth hour (also with an axle failure) and Hawthorn's Ferrari at around the same time with a broken piston. Neither of the Aston DBR1s reached the halfway mark, Salvadori's breaking its clutch and Brooks's car retired off the road with a seized gearbox in the night when running second.

Before he retired from the race Mike Hawthorn became the first driver to break the four-minute barrier in race conditions, lapping his Ferrari in 3 min 58.7 sec (203.015 km/h (126.15 mph)), and — due to impending changes in the regulations — this would not be broken for five years.

Ron Flockhart and Ivor Bueb were pretty well on the pace from the start, their ex-works Ecurie Ecosse Jaguar shadowing the Italian cars, and moved easily into the lead in the third hour. The 3.8 litre engine worked well, although Duncan Hamilton (with the American, Masten Gregory) lost time in his 3.8 litre car with a broken exhaust system and could only finish sixth.

Almost inevitably the race turned into a Jaguar rout and at the finish they were first, second, third, fourth . . . and sixth, the

Ninian Sanderson boards the Ecurie Ecosse Jaguar D-type which won in 1956, co-driven by Ron Flockhart. The following year Flockhart won again for the Scottish team, partnered by Ivor Bueb (A. Whyte).

interloper being Stuart Lewis-Evans's 3.8 litre Ferrari 290. It was the second victory in succession for Ecurie Ecosse, reinforced this time by second place overall claimed by the 3.4 litre D-type of Ninian Sanderson and John Lawrence.

At the end of the 1957 season the FIA introduced new rules, with a maximum capacity of 3,000 cc on all sports cars. This suited Ferrari down to the ground and no fewer than 10 Testa Rossas took the start, seven of them privately entered, all powered by V12 engines. The capacity limit suited Aston Martin very well too, the Feltham company's engines having been of 3 litre capacity for some years, and Jaguar produced a special 3 litre version of the straight-six for Duncan Hamilton, who again entered his car privately with Ivor Bueb. Ecurie Ecosse, however, developed their own 3 litre engines, bored and stroked versions of the 2.4 litre XK unit, and both retired in the first hour with piston failures.

Stirling Moss and Jack Brabham looked strong early in the race, the Englishman leading until the engine failed, and later on the Salvadori/Lewis-Evans DBR1 went off the road, and the Brooks/Trintignant Aston broke its transmission when lying third. Ferrari's chances tumbled when accidents sidelined the Testa Rossas of Willy Mairesse, Jerry Juhan, Gurney/Kessler and von Trips/Seidel, but

Second to the winning Jaguar in 1955 was the Aston Martin DB3S of Peter Collins and Paul Frère, the Belgian waiting for the last refuelling to be completed (Autosport).

Above left *Ferrari arrived in force for scrutineering in 1959 with seven Testa Rossas — none of which finished — and with four customer 250 GT models which earned third to sixth places* (Autosport).

Left *Porsche's new 550 RSK had an auspicious Sarthe debut in 1958 with third, fourth and fifth places in the classification. Victory, though, was still a dozen years away* (Porsche).

Above *After ten years in the front rank, Aston Martin finally 'cracked' Le Mans with a fine 1-2 victory in 1959. The winning Roy Salvadori/Carroll Shelby DBR/1 leads the sister car of Maurice Trintignant/ Paul Frère at the Esses early in the race* (Autosport).

Olivier Gendebien and Phil Hill kept up a lively duel with the Jaguar of Hamilton and Bueb throughout the night.

Intermittent rain improved Hamilton's chances, and he was still in with a chance of victory when he overturned his car on Sunday morning, swerving in heavy rain to avoid a slow-moving backmarker. It was to be the first of four Le Mans victories for the Belgian, Gendebien.

Second place, in the end, was claimed by the Aston Martin DB3S of brothers Graham and Peter Whitehead, the same car also having been second in 1955. This could so easily have been Aston Martin's success, had the DBR1s kept going to the end. Third, fourth and fifth were the 1½ litre Porsche RSKs, that of Jean Behra/Hans Herrmann being less than two laps behind the Whitehead Aston at the finish.

A head-to-head, Ferrari versus Aston Martin, was the menu for 1959, and after a decade of effort the rewards came to the British team. No fewer than seven Ferrari Testa Rossas were entered, and none of them finished: four broke their gearboxes, one had fuel starvation, and the two that lasted longest both had head gasket failures. On the other hand there were four Ferrari 250 GT models in the Grand Touring class and they all finished safely, and solidly in the third to sixth positions.

David Brown was now concentrating on his shortlived Formula 1

Above *Carroll Shelby at the wheel of the victorious Aston Martin DBR/1 in 1959. The reduction in engine capacity, to 3 litres, suited the British firm perfectly (*Autosport*).*

Opposite *The team that broke the mould. Ferrari's dominance at Le Mans was finally smashed by the American Ford team in 1966, and this picture taken minutes before the start captures the charged atmosphere (*Ford*).*

programme, but sent four DBR1 models to Le Mans. Once again Stirling Moss was the early leader, and once again his engine broke, this time on Sunday evening. The Whitehead/Naylor Aston was driven conservatively, but still left the road after four hours of racing.

Roy Salvadori and Carroll Shelby, backed by Maurice Trintignant and Paul Frère, lasted well. Only one Jaguar was entered, by Innes Ireland and Masten Gregory, and that retired from second place after six hours with a broken piston, but from the Ferrari camp Olivier Gendebien and Phil Hill kept up tremendous pressure, moving past the Astons in the night and looking ever more secure on Sunday morning. Shortly before midday, though, the red car slowed, and clouds of steam erupted as it stopped at its pit. The head gasket had blown, and the way was clear for Salvadori and the Texan, Shelby, to record their long-sought victory.

This ended a golden era, arguably the best in the history of the race. The inter-marque rivalries were certainly stronger in the 1950s than at any other time, and Jaguar, Mercedes, Ferrari and Aston Martin created reputations that never dimmed. Yet when we look back on the period, many people immediately recall the disaster of 1955. It can never be forgotten.

Left *The thundering Ford Mk 2 7 litre driven by New Zealanders Bruce McLaren and Chris Amon passes the pits on the way to victory in 1966 (Ford).*

Above *Chris Amon, winner in 1966 with Ford, switched to Ferrari the following year without success. He is rounding Tertre Rouge in the 4 litre, V12 P4 Spyder (Autosport).*

Right *Sunday morning at Indianapolis, and even the gendarme is wide awake as the Bruce McLaren/Mark Donohue Ford passes by on its way to fourth place (Ford).*

Chapter 5

The 1960s: Challenge to Ferrari

B ETWEEN 1960 and 1965 Enzo Ferrari's sports cars won the 24-hour race of Le Mans six times in succession, a record that would not be beaten until two decades later, by Porsche. It also took the Italian company to nine outright successes in the event, another record that would stand for nearly 20 years. The effort was all the more impressive since Ferrari was giving his priority to Grand Prix racing, enabling Phil Hill and Wolfgang von Trips to take the leading positions in the World Championship of 1961 and John Surtees to become the World Champion in 1964, so this was surely the finest era in Ferrari's history.

It was all the more impressive that Ferrari's programmes were entirely different, the Formula 1 effort concentrating on the 2.5 litre V6 engine in 1960, and on the 1.5 litre 'Dino' engine until 1965, while the sports cars were powered by the Gioacchino Colombo–designed V12 engines, evolved from the 1.5 litre of 1947 and developed in higher capacities by Aurelio Lampredi. One new design followed another in the Sports and Grand Touring categories, and even a change of formula in 1962 failed to halt Ferrari's string of successes; neither did a change of top management at the end of 1961, nor rather lightweight opposition from the Camoradi Maseratis, which were fast but fragile.

For the 1960 season, which consisted of merely five races, of which Le Mans was the last, Ferrari developed the TR60 model from the Testa Rossa. The 3 litre V12 engine was dry-sumped so that it could be positioned lower in the chassis, a new four-speed transmission was developed, and for the 24-hour race three of the works cars had coil-sprung independent rear suspensions, a familiar feature, while two had experimental de Dion rear suspensions, which proved to be 50 kg (110 lb) heavier; all five of them developed 300 bhp, with

Left *The Hans Herrmann/ Richard Attwood Porsche 917 was not only colourful in 1970, but also successful. A 4.5 litre back-up car, it was entered by Porsche Salzburg (*Autosport*).*

In the North American Racing Team Ferrari Testa Rossa, Ricardo Rodriguez made his Le Mans début at the age of 18 and astonished everyone by finishing second, with André Pilette (Autosport).

six twin-choke Weber carburettors.

Backing these were seven privately–entered 250 GT models, magnificent machines with triple carburated V12 engines, also of 3 litre capacity, developing 270 bhp. A dozen of the 55 starters were made in Maranello, and their presence was quite formidable. Fuel tank capacities of the sports-prototype models were restricted to 140 litres (30.8 gallons) but the minimum distance between refuelling stops, previously 30 laps, was scrapped . . . which was just as well, for Ferrari!

Aston Martin had withdrawn from sports car racing to concentrate on its faltering Formula 1 programme, but there were two privately–entered DBR1 models taking part in the 24-hours, one for Jim Clark and Roy Salvadori, another entered by the Scottish Border Reivers team for Ian Baillie and Jack Fairman. Jaguar was represented by two privately–entered, short-stroke, 3 litre D-types, one from Ecurie Ecosse for Ron Flockhart/Ivor Bueb and another entered by Briggs Cunningham — who had now abandoned his ambition to win the race with an American car — for Dan Gurney and Walt Hansgen. Cunningham also entered a pair of Chevrolet Corvettes, one for himself and Bill Kimberley, the other for Bob Grossmann and John Fitch, but these were in the GT class and looked anything but competitive.

At this stage, Porsche was still running in the 1,600 cc class, and

Little and large! The 4.6 litre V8 Camoradi Chevrolet Corvette thunders past the Index of Thermal Efficiency winning DB Panhard of Laureau and Armagnac. With a 702 cc engine, the French car was fifteenth overall, covering 2,116 miles (Autosport).

despite winning the Sebring 12-hours and the Targa Florio, could not be expected to do well at Le Mans where 'cubic inches' and power mattered above all. If there was any realistic opposition, it came from the Camoradi team Maserati tipo 61s, one of which, driven by Stirling Moss and Dan Gurney, had won the Nürburgring 1,000 Km.

The season was clearly not going Ferrari's way, despite having won the opening round at Buenos Aires, but Le Mans would surely be another matter, for the Maseratis were unlikely to go the distance.

After winning the World F1 Championship with the famous 250F in 1957 'the other Modena company', namely Maserati, had got into serious financial difficulties and, like Alfa Romeo, had to be rescued by the Italian government. The brilliant design director, Ing Giulio Alfieri, kept the company in competitions with the ageing 200SI 2 litre sports car. He then designed one of the most intriguing cars of the period, the tipo 60, with a complex steel-tube chassis. Made up of around 200 lengths of mild steel it resembled, according to critics, a cat's cradle, a plate of spaghetti . . . or a birdcage, and it was the last name that gained currency. The Birdcage Maserati!

Initially it was powered by the company's 2 litre, four cylinder engine eventually producing 200 bhp, and Stirling Moss tested it in this form at the Nürburgring prior to racing his Aston Martin in June 1959. The English driver thought it handled better than any car he had driven before and made a number of suggestions that might turn it into a world-beater, and a month later he drove the tipo 60 to victory in the 2 litre sports car supporting race at Rouen.

The tipo 60 was all Alfieri's work, including the engine development, the 'transaxle' transmission later copied by Alfa Romeo and Porsche, the de Dion rear suspension (based, like the front suspension, on that of the 250F), the body design, even the huge disc brakes based on a Girling design, which made it the best braked car in competitions.

Moss's principal recommendation was to turn the tipo 60 into a 3 litre, and to find much more power. Then, he said, it would be capable of winning races outright. Maserati boss Omer Orsi saw the logic, but declared that the company did not have the resources to undertake a programme.

Alfieri duly enlarged the engine to 3 litres by increasing the height of the block, but there were serious vibrational problems and the engine exploded on the dynomometer. He then changed the bore/stroke ratio to reach a cylinder volume of 2,890 cc and the engine worked very well, though it developed only 250 bhp. Even so the chassis weighed just 30 kg (66lb), and the whole car weighed 520 kg (1,144 lb), saving 180 kg (396 lb) compared with the Ferrari TR and Aston Martin DBR1 models. On power-to-weight it had the edge.

And who would race these cars? Maserati laid down a batch of six customer cars, all sold to Americans, and by the time they were delivered in 1959/60 most had been converted to tipo 61, 2.9 litre specification. One, not yet a customer, had the idealistic ambition of winning the World Sports Car Championship, and Lloyd 'Lucky' Casner, from Miami, began to put his plan together in the autumn of 1959. He was a used-car salesman, claimed to be rich, and was regarded by many Americans as a con-man. At the time the Goodyear Tire Company was trying to shake off a stodgy image and was looking for ways of competing with Firestone, which had a virtual monopoly of American racing. Casner heard of this, and managed to secure from Goodyear the promise of $50,000 for the 1960 season, plus a towing truck. With that he flew to Italy and put together a deal for two cars (one of which, the Rouen–winning tipo 60 converted to take the larger engine, cost $6,500), and Maserati agreed to provide technical back-up.

Casner raced his cars under the Camoradi banner, an acronym for Casner Motor Racing Division, and with Aston Martin's withdrawal he was able to hire the likes of Stirling Moss, Dan Gurney, Carroll Shelby, Masten Gregory and Jo Bonnier, a fine team. Casner himself had little racing experience and lacked driving ability, although he would drive on occasions. The establishment was extremely wary of him, but he was, perhaps, merely 20 years ahead of his time in entrepreneurial vision.

The Camoradi Maseratis were certainly fast and worried Ferrari considerably. They led easily at Buenos Aires, Sebring and in the Targa Florio, only to be put out by assorted failures, but Moss and Gurney had a triumphant outing at the Nürburgring and Casner felt confident about Le Mans too.

There were three Camoradi Maseratis in the race and one of them, for Masten Gregory and Chuck Daigh, had a streamlined windscreen that was the talk of the paddock. The regulations demanded screens 25 cm (10 in) in height, something that would slow the Ferraris down quite a bit to around 160 mph (257 km/h). For the quickest Maserati, timed at 169 mph (271.7 km/h), Alfieri designed a screen that extended a long way forward, over the engine and almost to the front of the car; it was about 60 in (150 cm) long and, sure enough, it came up to the drivers' eye level to meet the height requirement. A long tail was designed as well, and the tipo 60 was without question the fastest car on the track.

Moss had priced himself out of Casner's budget, Shelby left the team after a financial disagreement, and Gurney signed up to drive Briggs Cunningham's Jaguar, so Camoradi was short of drivers. Italian drivers Gino Munaron and Giorgio Scarlatti were recommended by Maserati for the second car, with a long tail, and the third, in normal trim, was driven by Casner with Jim Jeffords.

Gregory had trouble starting his car after the 'run and jump' start and 23 cars were surging under the Dunlop Bridge before he got going, but he had overtaken the lot by the time he reached Mulsanne Corner! He led the first lap by four seconds, and simply drove away from the Ferraris to the extent that he had lapped all of them within two hours.

It was a sensational start, but when Daigh climbed in he could not get the starter to work. It was buried in a mass of tubes, and an hour went by before the starter could be replaced so he went from first to forty-sixth place. Two of the works Ferraris were out, though, von Trips and Scarfiotti running out of fuel on the course, and Gendebien was just able to coast into his pit, out of fuel, after 22 laps. The scarlet cars were using much more fuel than had been anticipated, perhaps due to changing the exhaust system after the trials weekend.

Munaron's Maserati retired on the course when smoke poured from the engine compartment, though it transpired later that the starter motor had burned out. Casner's starter motor was then changed as a precaution, but during a wet and foggy evening he buried the car in the sandbank at Mulsanne, and had to retire with jammed gear selection. That just left one car, the Gregory/Daigh 'Streamliner'. This was tenth and picking up places nicely when the rear wheels lost grip on the soaking track and allowed the engine to over-rev. Daigh, too, was out of the race.

Both Jaguars retired, Gurney's with a blown piston and Flockhart's with a broken crankshaft, and that left two Aston Martins to combat a horde of Ferraris.

Olivier Gendebien and Paul Frère commanded the race once Gregory's Maserati was out of the way, and they were pursued throughout by Ricardo Rodriguez and André Pilette. Jim Clark and Roy Salvadori ran the Ferraris hard during the night, when it poured with rain, but found themselves outpaced when the weather cleared up on Sunday and finished third, 11 laps behind the winners. Then came four Ferrari 250 GTs — covered by 23 km (14.3 miles), or two laps — the Fitch/Grossmann Corvette, and the Baillie/Fairman Aston Martin which had spent time in the pits.

Although the Camoradi Maserati team had led all the races and won at the 'Ring, Goodyear was far from satisfied and delivered Casner an ultimatum to win the Sebring 12-Hours in 1961, or lose his sponsorship. Stirling Moss and Graham Hill were hired to race the new tipo 63, in which the engine was transferred to the back of the car without radically redesigning the chassis, while Casner and Gregory handled the tipo 61. Moss and Hill immediately disliked the 63, which did not handle so well, and realized that its rear suspension was too weak for Sebring's bumpy surface, so they switched to the tipo 61 . . . which lost two laps at the start with flooded carburettors. Gregory, meanwhile, drove the tipo 63 far faster than in practice to lead the race for four laps, only to begin to lose ground as the rear chassis tubes started to crack up.

After two hours the Moss/Hill car retired with a broken exhaust manifold, and the tipo 63 soon followed it into retirement, effectively ending Goodyear's backing of Camoradi into the bargain. Ferrari made a clean sweep of the Sebring results with TR61 models, similar to the previous year's but with more aerodynamic bodywork which engineering chief Carlo Chiti had designed with wind tunnel assistance. A new Ferrari model was the mid-engined 246SP, which followed Formula 1 practice in placing the 2.4 litre V6 Dino engine ahead of the rear wheels, and in this car von Trips and Gendebien won the Targa Florio race, next in the 1961 championship.

Casner took his car to the Nürburgring for a film exercise but had no money to race it, until the organizers put together a package that paid for fuel and mechanics. There were no spare wheels or tyres, but Masten Gregory set off in dreadfully wet weather conditions and comfortably ran in fifth place, gradually moving up as the Ferraris and Porsches ran into difficulties. Casner held on to third place during his stint, and Gregory inherited the lead when the engine seized on Moss's Porsche, and Phil Hill went off the road in his Ferrari.

Two laps from the end Gregory stopped for some fuel and Casner saw that the Maserati's tyres were bald, but the track was dry and he advised Gregory to take it easy, and finish on the rims if need be. The Maserati earned its last major international victory, from the Ferrari TR61 driven by the Rodriguez brothers — and an hour later the left rear tyre exploded while the car was sitting in its garage!

Casner had no backing to enter cars at Le Mans, returned his tipo 63 to the factory, and drove his tipo 61 in a couple of minor races.

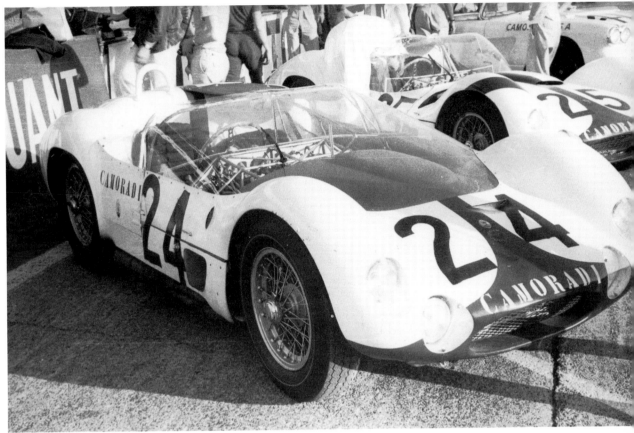

*The two Camoradi team 'Bird-
cage' Maseratis lined up in front
of the pits before the start in
1960, and behind them the
team's Chevrolet Corvette. Masten Gregory and Chuck Daigh
drove number 24 which was
timed as the fastest car on the
Mulsanne Straight, at 273
km/h. Neither car finished
(Haymarket Motoring Photo
Library).*

Maserati, instead, came to an arrangement with Briggs Cunningham
for Le Mans and two of the cars, tipo 63s, were run with Maserati's
own 3 litre V12 engine while Cunningham drove a 2 litre tipo 60.
Augie Pabst and Dr Dick Thompson drove steadily and quietly to
fourth place behind a trio of Ferraris, Walt Hansgen and Bruce
McLaren retired with accident damage, while in the Scuderia
Serenissima car Scarfiotti and Vaccarella retired during the evening
with a blown head gasket. Cunningham finished eighth in the 2 litre
model, with Bill Kimberley, and Maserati's international career
seemed to be at an end.

The Le Mans 24-Hours Race was again won by the Belgian driver
Olivier Gendebien with Phil Hill, repeating the pairing's success of
1958. Very strong opposition came from Ricardo and Pedro Rodriguez in the NART Ferrari TR61. The combined ages of the two
Mexicans was 39, less than the age of a good many more experienced drivers in the race, and they battled away for the lead for 22
hours, until a piston collapsed. The Ferrari 246SP of Richie Ginther/
Wolfgang von Trips acquitted itself very well, always in the top three
or four positions until Sunday morning when it ran out of fuel on the
course.

At the end of the year Carlo Chiti and team manager Romolo Tavoni left Ferrari, acrimoniously, to set up the ATS Formula 1 team. Chief engineers Franco Rocchi (chassis) and Walter Salvarani (engines) were to be assisted by young engineers Mauro Forghieri and Angelo Bellei, and Eugenio Dragoni was appointed team manager . . . a man who seemed to live up to his name, for in the next three years he effectively sacked Phil Hill and John Surtees, always preferring Italian drivers.

The FIA had announced, early in 1961, that the '62 Championship would be for Grand Touring cars, but later relented and allowed 'Experimental' cars to take part, even raising the maximum engine capacity to 4 litres. This was *carte blanche* for a manufacturer like Ferrari, who resurrected the Lampredi improved 'America' 4 litre engine and installed it in the Testa Rossa chassis. This model became the 330LM and only one was entered, for Gendebien and Phil Hill. It was easily the fastest car on the course but also the most experimental. The Modena company also entered or supported a 246

British production sports cars supported Le Mans in great numbers, deriving valuable publicity. The Sunbeam Alpine of Peter Harper and Peter Proctor finished fifteenth in 1962, covering 2,237 miles (Haymarket).

for the Rodriguez brothers, a new V8 mid-engined car for Baghetti and Scarfiotti, and a 4 litre version of the 250 GT for Mike Parkes and Lorenzo Bandini. This was a mixed bag in an experimental year, and with interesting opposition.

Now finished with Formula 1, Aston Martin entered a Project 212 for Graham Hill and Richie Ginther, with a bored-out 4 litre engine and independent (Lagonda) rear suspension. Maserati was persuaded to return to the GT category by French importer Colonel André Simon, presenting three tipo 151 models.

Jaguar returned, too, with three lightweight E-types with 3.8 litre engines, though all were privately entered in the GT category, and there was nothing on the horizon to trouble a Ferrari walkover . . . barring mechanical failures, of course.

Graham Hill led the opening lap in the Aston P212 before being overwhelmed by the Ferraris, but he and Ginther ran strongly for three hours until electrical problems intervened, and the engine failed. Gendebien and Phil Hill, driving as slowly and carefully as they could, were then harried by the Rodriguez brothers in the 246SP, which finally retired on Sunday morning with broken transmission. Then the new V8 engined 268SP continued the chase until it, too, succumbed to a broken gearbox, and nothing but a failing clutch stood between Gendebien, Hill and another victory. The Belgian had won for the fourth time, an all-time record in 1962, and he then announced his retirement from competitions.

The Maseratis acquitted themselves well, though they failed to last. The Thompson/Kimberley entry went off the road in the sixth hour, having run as high as second overall, the Trintignant/Lucien Bianchi entry retired in the night with broken rear suspension, and Hansgen/McLaren went out on Sunday morning due to engine failure.

The GT class was very easily won by Guichet and Noblet who were second overall in their 3 litre Ferrari GTO, more than 100 km (62 miles) ahead of 'Elde' and 'Beurlys' in their similar GTO, while third and fourth were the two Jaguar E-type GTs of Briggs Cunningham/Bill Kimberley and Peter Lumsden/Peter Sargent.

A new sound filled the air in 1963, the shrill whistle and whooshing noise of a jet engine! Back in 1953 the innovative Automobile Club de l'Ouest had offered a 25,000 franc prize for the first jet-engined car to finish the race and ten years later the Rover company rose to the challenge. The Solihull firm, lacking racing experience, asked BRM for technical assistance and the car was, in fact, a widened version of the World Championship–winning Formula 1 car, with sports bodywork. It was driven by Graham Hill and Richie Ginther.

The Rover-BRM did not have a heat exchanger and was thirsty on fuel, but the ACO allowed it to run outside the regulations and qualify for the special prize, but not for overall classification. Hill and Ginther had the starting number 00, and started 20 seconds after the field had departed. They had a completely trouble-free run and covered 4,172

A new sight, a new sound in 1963. Rover commissioned BRM to build a turbine-powered car to earn a special prize of 25,000 Francs offered by the Automobile Club de l'Ouest. Although running outside the main competition (numbered 00) Graham Hill, pictured, and Richie Ginther covered 2,593 miles and finished ahead of the seventh placed AC Cobra (Auto-sport).

km (2,593 miles), enough to have been classified in seventh place.

Another significant car in the race was Eric Broadley's Lola GT, an attractive coupé built in a small workshop in Bromley, south of London. Powered by a 4.7 litre Ford stock-block V8 (and taking advantage of the removal of an upper limit on capacity for 'experimental' cars), the Lola had raced only once before, at the Nürburgring, and arrived late for scrutineering. Again the ACO relaxed the regulations and allowed David Hobbs and Richard Attwood to qualify and race, and after a steady start the Lola had moved up to eighth place by midnight.

Difficulties with the Colotti transmission slowed the Lola's progress during the night, and eventually caused Hobbs to crash at the Esses in the fifteenth hour of the race. The mid-engined GT prototype had shown remarkable promise, especially in handling, and impressed Ford's hierarchy. So, too, did the performance of the Ford supported AC Cobras, a 4.7 litre development of the AC Ace dreamed up by Carroll Shelby for the GT class. They were not technically advanced by any means, their traditional shapes restricting speeds on the Mulsanne Straight, but one of them driven by Bolton and Sanderson finished in seventh place, the fourth GT home after a trio of Ferraris.

The boom of the American V8 engines was the future of Le Mans, and the latent challenge to Ferrari. As yet the Italians had no inkling that Ford would mount serious efforts in the future, taking the top six positions in 1963 and brushing aside the challenges from Maserati and Aston Martin as mere irritants. Aston Martin was there for the last time, as a works team managed by John Wyer, with the potent Zagato–bodied Project 215 handled by Lucien Bianchi and Phil Hill. The Aston had a spaceframe chassis, in which the engine was mounted 200 mm (8 in) further back, located a 'transaxle' gearbox at the rear, and was timed at 187 mph (300 km/h) on the long straight. It was quick, certainly, but trailed the Ferraris and retired in the third hour with a broken driveshaft.

The single Maserati tipo 151 was fast, too, with its 5 litre V8 Maserati engine and de Dion rear suspension, and André Simon gallantly led the race for two hours . . . the Ferraris watched and waited, and when Lucky Casner took over from Simon the gearbox broke.

Ferrari presented yet another combination for the race in 1963, putting the V12 engine behind the cockpit in the three works cars. In removing the upper capacity limit the FIA also imposed a sliding scale of weights, and Ferrari decided to revert to 3 litre capacity for the Testa Rossa power units although Pedro Rodriguez and Roger Penske drove the previous year's winner, the front-engined 4 litre model, for Luigi Chinetti's North American Racing Team.

With the Aston Martin and Maserati opposition sidelined in the early stages, Ferrari absolutely dominated the race, John Surtees/Willy Mairesse leading Mike Parkes/Umberto Maglioli and Lodovico Scarfiotti/Lorenzo Bandini. Their challenge now came from the NART team, but Rodriguez and Penske were hampered by tyre problems and retired before midnight when an oil line broke, causing the car to spin on its own oil.

Parkes and Maglioli lost time with an ignition problem, while 'Beurlys' and Langlois, in the class-winning GTO, were delayed from the start by fuel feed problems. Both crews had to work hard throughout the night to make up time, but the two-lap lead established by Surtees and Mairesse was dashed mid-morning on Sunday just after a refuelling stop. Petrol had overflowed into the undertray, and the first time Mairesse used the brakes, at the Esses, the car burst into flames and was burned out.

Scarfiotti and Bandini inherited a huge lead, and became the first all-Italian crew to win the 24-hour race. It was the first success for a mid-engined car, too, and 134 km (83 miles) behind them came Beurlys' Ferrari GTO merely 75 m (82 yd) ahead of the Parkes/Maglioli 250P. It was the first time in the history of the race that a single make had claimed the top six finishing places, the previous best result for a make having been in 1957 when Jaguar D-types finished in the first four positions, and sixth.

Henry Ford, chairman of the international company, proposed to

Ford's assault on Le Mans began in 1964 with the new GT40 design, which proved fragile in the engine and transmission departments. Phil Hill, pictured, broke Surtees' Ferrari lap record by 4 sec, establishing it at 3 min 49.2 sec before retiring. Following is the Salmon/ Sutcliffe Aston Martin DB4 Zagato which also retired (Ford).

buy Ferrari outright in 1963. Discussions took place but few people seriously expected Enzo Ferrari to sell out to Americans, and in due course his manufacturing business was taken over by Fiat, a much more suitable marriage, while Ferrari retained control of his racing programme. Ford was, at that time, heavily engaged in its 'total performance' programme, and soon made victory at Le Mans (and Daytona, Sebring and other prestige events) its top priority. Ford's saloon cars were made ever faster, rallies were tackled successfully, and by 1967 Ford's money had paid for the Cosworth DFV, without doubt the most brilliant race engine design ever conceived.

Straight after Le Mans, the Americans set up the Ford Advanced Vehicles company at Slough. It was directed by Roy Lunn, an expatriate Englishman working in Detroit, and managed by John Wyer, who could see Aston Martin's interests waning. Eric Broadley was engaged under a 12-month contract as a freelance designer to develop the new Ford GT car, and John Horsman was the chief engineer. It was a close-knit team formed with a purpose, and although there were political problems the new GT duly appeared at the Le Mans trials in 1964. It was called the GT40, since it stood 40 in high.

The GT40 was initially powered by Ford's aluminium 4.2 litre V8 engine, basically a production unit with a central camshaft and pushrods, but developed sufficiently to take Jim Clark to second place in the '63 Indianapolis 500. (Later, he and Graham Hill would win the Indy race with similar engines.)

With four Weber carburettors the pushrod engine developed 350 bhp, and the Colotti gearbox would prove the car's Achilles' heel, until the 1965 season when a new ZF transmission became available. Both GT40s were crashed in wet weather at the Le Mans trials, but at the Nürburgring Phil Hill made an excellent practice time at little over nine minutes, and went well in the race until the rear suspension broke. It had been a useful experience.

Three Ford GT40s were entered for Le Mans, providing the principal opposition for Ferrari's fleet of mid-engined 275P (3.3 litre) and 330P (4 litre) prototypes. Backing the American effort was a pair of more aerodynamic, coupé–bodied AC Cobra Ford Daytonas, to give them their full title, Dan Gurney and Bob Bondurant in one, which finished fourth overall, and Chris Amon/Jochen Neerpasch in the other which retired with electrical difficulties.

Richie Ginther and Masten Gregory were the Ford team's 'hares' and led from the start with the Surtees/Bandini Ferrari leading the red pack in pursuit. Phil Hill and Bruce McLaren were delayed by carburation problems but began to move up steadily, while Richard Attwood and Jo Schlesser ran nicely around fifth place until a fuel line parted company in the fifth hour, causing a minor fire which put them out of the race. Soon afterwards the Ginther/Gregory GT40 forfeited second place when the gearbox broke, and after dawn on Sunday Hill and McLaren also retired with a broken gearbox, having moved up to fourth place. Hill had established a new lap record at 3 min 49.2 sec, breaking the Ferrari record set by John Surtees in 1963 by a clear four seconds. While lapping at 131.7 mph (212 km/h), Hill's car was timed at 191 mph (307.4 km/h) on the Mulsanne Straight, showing that the GT40 had enormous potential that would take another year to develop.

Jean Guichet and Nino Vaccarella won that race for Ferrari, their 3.3 litre 275P model beating the more powerful but 100 kg (220 lb) heavier 4 litre 330P models of Graham Hill/Jo Bonnier and Surtees/Bandini. In fourth place, though, was the thundering AC Cobra Coupé of Dan Gurney and Bob Bondurant, narrowly beating a pair of Ferrari GTOs to win the Grand Touring Category. Half a dozen Porsche 904s filled out the top 12 places, new 2 litre models in the GT class powered by four-cylinder Carrera engines. Two eight-cylinder versions of the 904 were entered by the factory, and were heading for good placings when eliminated by clutch and electrical problems.

Above *Ford returned in 1965 with a pair of 7-litre Mark 2 models, which both broke their transmissions. The Bruce McLaren/Ken Miles entry led the Ferraris for two hours before its gearbox broke (Ford).*

Right *Porsche's 906 six-cylinder model fared well in 1966 taking fourth to seventh places behind the mighty Fords. This one though, driven by Peter Gregg and Sten Axelsson, was a last-hour retirement with a broken rocker arm (Porsche).*

Ferrari had been unable to homologate the LM model as a Grand Touring model and had even handed in his entrant's licence in a fit of pique (which did not last very long!) when the FIA refused to homologate the car when enough parts had been made to construct 100 examples. The 275LM, therefore, continued to run in the prototype class as a back-up to the factory's 4 litre, 330 P2 models in 1965, and the GTO model was further developed with the 3.3 litre engine, becoming the GT Berlinetta (GTB).

Ford, too, experienced political problems, the hierarchy having expected a quick result. The main programme was moved to the States, where the Shelby American organization carried out development work at Ford's Kar Kraft division in Detroit. Working on the time-honoured principle that 'there's no substitute for cubic inches', Shelby reworked the car to accept Ford's iron-block 7 litre engine, a production unit that developed close on 500 bhp. In Slough, Ford Advanced Vehicles was later taken over by John Wyer and John Willment, who formed the JW Automotive company, and their brief was to develop the GT40 model and to build 100 examples for homologation into the GT category. Some were prepared for road use, but the majority of the 105 actually made were raced in many parts of the world.

Wyer's GT40 switched to the iron-block 4.7 litre engine which developed 380 bhp, though five years later, and towards the end of the GT40's competitions life, it had been developed to the region of 500 bhp with full 5 litre capacity, fuel injection, dry sumping, Gurney Weslake cylinder heads and other detail modifications. It was the best investment Ford made, though the company did not realize this at the time . . . Shelby was given the job of winning races outright, the big prestige job, and JW Automotive would take care of the Grand Touring class.

The season began well as Ken Miles and Lloyd Ruby won the Daytona Continental race in their Ford Mark II, as the 7 litre version was called, and on arrival at Le Mans Shelby's team showed its hand when Phil Hill made the best practice time at 3 min 33 sec (142.25 mph (228.9 km/h)), all of 16 seconds quicker than he had gone the year before in the GT40!

Ferrari had prepared new cars with 3.3 and 4.0 litre engines developing 330 bhp and 410 bhp respectively. The P2 models now used the V12 as a stressed member and technical director Mauro Forghieri had virtually redesigned the engines, which now had twin overhead camshafts on each bank and four valves per cylinder.

'Lucky' Casner, briefly a prominent figure on the scene, lost his life when he crashed André Simon's Maserati during qualifying, and the new mid-engined tipo 65 for Jo Siffert and Jochen Neerpasch did not even last one lap of the race. That ended Maserati's direct involvement at Le Mans on a low note, with 26 starts in 12 years but only four finishes, the best of which was the fourth place claimed by Augie Pabst and Dick Thompson in 1961.

A-hunting we will go . . . a pair of 7 litre Fords go Ferrari chasing, and under extreme pressure a dozen assorted Ferraris retired, leaving only one Berlinetta in eighth place (Ford).

Back in Modena, Enzo Ferrari might have slept well on the night of the race. Before darkness fell on Saturday evening the entire Ford Mark II and GT40 challenge was out of the event with assorted head gasket and gearbox failures. The Mark IIs had been fast, of course, Bruce McLaren/Ken Miles and Phil Hill/Chris Amon taking charge from the start, but Hill's clutch started slipping in the second hour, and eventually failed in the evening. McLaren's gearbox broke in the third hour, Shelby lost his two GT40s with head gasket failures, and so did Wyer's team. All too soon Ferrari was unchallenged, although the new six and eight-cylinder Porsche 904s were going extremely fast, and were as reliable as usual.

During the night Ferrari's dominance began to look shaky, as all five P2s went through a spate of cracked brake discs. New internally–ventilated discs broke one after another in the cold night air, until Ferrari had no spares, but engines and gearboxes were the actual causes of retirement for four of them. Only one P2, the NART entry driven by Pedro Rodriguez and Nino Vaccarella, reached the finish in seventh position.

Ferrari's customers saved the day, Jochen Rindt and Masten Gregory taking a totally unexpected victory in the NART Ferrari 275LM ahead of the similar machine driven by Frenchmen Dumay and Gosselin. The 275 GTB of Mairesse and Gosselin finished third, winning the GT category and Porsche 904s were fourth and fifth. Down in tenth place, after the jet engine went off colour, was the

Ford tried to stage manage a tie, but based on relative starting positions the organizers put Bruce McLaren and Chris Amon (2) a dozen metres ahead of Ken Miles and Denny Hulme, with Bucknum and Hutcheson (5) third (Ford).

Rover-BRM driven by Graham Hill and Jackie Stewart.

No expense was spared by Ford in winning the race in 1966, mounting the largest and most costly effort ever seen. An army of mechanics and back-up personnel seemed to fill the paddock, a total of eight Mark IIs being entered by Shelby, Holman and Moody, and Alan Mann Racing in England. In their wake were five GT40s but, again, none would finish.

Ferrari responded with a trio of P3s, all 4 litre models with fuel injection and 420 bhp. But after a record-breaking six victories in succession it was the Italian company's turn to falter. The weekend started badly when the poor relationship between John Surtees and manager Dragoni finally fell apart, the Englishman quitting the team on the spot, and deteriorated as the P3s all retired. Scarfiotti was involved in a multiple accident during the night, Rodriguez and Ginther had their gearbox fail while in fourth place (they had usually been amongst the Fords, and had led for a while) and on Sunday morning Bandini and Guichet retired, also with a broken gearbox.

The Fords were not immune to problems either, but three of the seven finished safely and occupied the top three positions, McLaren and Amon attempting to dead-heat with Miles and Denny Hulme; the organizers gave the verdict to the New Zealanders, who had started the race further down the track. Third was the Mark II of Bucknum and Hutcheson, and behind them a quartet of six-cylinder Porsche 906s. This time Ferrari's customers could not save the day, but the

GT class was won by default by the 275 GTB driven by Piers Courage and Roy Pike.

The two leading Fords broke the distance record easily, covering 3,009 miles (4,842 km) in 24 hours, and Dan Gurney lowered the lap record to 3 min 30.2 sec in his Mark II, which retired with a blown head gasket on Sunday morning, having led much of the way.

The Chaparral was a new make in 1965, a project mounted by Jim Hall with covert support from General Motors, who supplied the 5.3 litre Chevrolet V8 engine and two-speed, clutchless transmission. In the hands of Phil Hill and Jo Bonnier the Chaparral 2D made an exploratory run, retiring before midnight with electrical failure, but two developed models, the 2F, returned in 1967 and caused a sensation. High above the rear wheels was a tilting wing, which was flat and feathered along the straight, when the driver's left foot depressed a pedal, but tilted forward to assist braking and cornering when the pedal was released. The 2F had already run in the Targa Florio, the sight of it passing into Sicilian folklore, and at the Nürburgring, and had led both races . . .

Ford's effort concentrated on the J-car, more familiarly the MkIV, which like the Chaparral had a production–based 7 litre V8 engine. Ferrari responded with a new top end on the V12 engine, having three valves per cylinder, the 4 litre engines now developing over 450 bhp, and the P4 was further developed with wider track measurements and 'faster' bodywork.

This was the race of the Titans, but it would be the last for a few years to feature such a variety of powerful machines. The FIA had announced new rules for 1968: prototypes would be restricted to 3 litre capacity and Sports Prototype cars (of which 50 had to be made) to 5 litres, the ruling body fondly believing that the latter category would include such cars as Lolas and Fords with stock-block engines.

In 1967, pole position was an arm-locking contest between Phil Hill in the Chaparral and Bruce McLaren in the Ford MkIV, McLaren claiming the fastest time by just 0.3 sec.

The Chaparrals started carefully, and the Ronnie Bucknum/Paul Hawkins Shelby Ford (an interim MkIIIB model) led for the first hour, only to be delayed by a broken water pipe; the car lasted until Sunday before the engine broke. Dan Gurney and A. J. Foyt, the USAC driver making his first and only appearance at Le Mans, drove what they determined to be the most careful race of their lives, lifting off well before anyone else at Mulsanne and saving the car in every possible way. Even so Gurney ran second to Bucknum in the first hour and took a lead that he never relinquished, adding more than 240 miles to the distance record by Sunday afternoon.

The Gurney/Foyt Ford was the only one to finish trouble-free, chased home by a pair of Ferrari P4s driven by Scarfiotti/Parkes and Mairesse/'Beurlys'. McLaren and Donohue finished fourth with clutch trouble but, before crashing out with brake failure, Mario Andretti lopped a massive 7 seconds off the lap record, lowering it to

A. J. Foyt only went to Le Mans once, and won! Partnering Dan Gurney, Foyt drove a very cautious race to preserve his Ford Mk IV to beat a pair of Ferrari P4 models. The result proved conclusively that Ferrari's era was finished, as Fords would win in '68 and '69 as well (Ford).

3 min 23.6 sec (147.89 mph (238 km/h)). With the track being revised the following year, and a new formula slowing down the cars, the record stands for all time.

As for the Chaparrals, the Jennings/Johnson entry went beyond midnight, never higher than thirteenth, before retiring with a starter motor failure, but Phil Hill and Mike Spence went well into Sunday morning before the transmission broke, having been right up with the Fords and Ferraris all night. Jim Hall's memorable European interlude finished on a high note with victory in the BOAC 500 Mile race at Brands Hatch, and then the team returned to the States to concentrate on Can-Am racing, and more futuristic designs.

More interesting cars in the race included a pair of Lola T70s with new Aston Martin V8 engines, and a pair of 2 litre BRM engined Matras, products of the French aerospace company. Lola's name would return to the forefront, although the Aston Martin engines were unready and unreliable on their debut, and Matra's reputation would climb ever higher in the 3 litre era.

The 1968 season was heralded by disappointment and debate. The American Fords and Chaparrals were certainly banished, but the JW Automotive GT40s qualified easily to run as homologated Sports cars, with more than 50 manufactured, and now with 4.9 litre engines. Eric Broadley's Lolas only just qualified when the Can-Am cars were counted up, while Porsche homologated the customer 906

A new era began in 1968 when the 3 litre prototype/5 litre GT formula was introduced. The Ford GT40 was superior at Le Mans, but Jo Siffert and Jochen Neerpasch gave the new Porsche 908 model a good Sarthe debut, finishing third overall (Porsche).

model and Ferrari the 275 LM. Just about everyone else would have to run in the 3 litre prototype category.

Inevitably there was a sense of anti-climax about the 1968 season, made stronger when strikes in France caused the 24-hour race to be postponed until September. Yet as the season went on it became clear that the contest was wide open and quite fascinating, John Wyer's Gulf-sponsored GT40 team holding its own against the new Porsche 908s which were lighter and more nimble, but not yet reliable. The Sports category in which the GT40s were homologated allowed a minimum weight of 800 kg (1,764 lb), but there was (at that time) no minimum weight for the prototypes, and the following year Porsche would make some special, ultra-light 908 models for such races as the Targa Florio and the Nürburgring.

Alfa Romeo's Autodelta division, now headed by Carlo Chiti, produced the interesting T33 model, though initially with a 2 litre V8 engine, and Renault produced a 3 litre V8 engine for the Alpine A220 model, though it never looked powerful or competitive. Wyer's team was also developing the Mirage chassis on its own account for the prototype class, the power unit to be either a Ford Cosworth DFV or BRM V12; and Len Bailey, with substantial assistance from Ford, was occupied in designing the futuristic P68 prototype coupé for Alan Mann, which would be powered by the Cosworth V8, and was one of the most promising designs.

The Cosworth DFV had already begun to establish a clear superiority in Formula 1 racing, for which it already developed 410 bhp. Superficially, therefore, Porsche's new air-cooled 908 engine with two valves per cylinder, seemed to have a major disadvantage with 330 bhp, although in 1969 this was increased to 360 bhp. Porsche's chassis were always the lightest, though, and lap speeds

Alfa Romeo returned to competitions with the 2 litre tipo 33 model, and did extremely well in 1968 to collect fourth, fifth and sixth places overall (Alfa Romeo).

often compared well with Formula 1 times.

Early in the 1968 season, Porsche relied upon their 2.2 litre 907 models to overwhelm lightweight opposition at Daytona and Sebring. But in the BOAC 500 at Brands Hatch Jacky Ickx and Brian Redman drove the JWA Gulf-Ford GT40 superbly to finish ahead of the factory 907s handled by Gerhard Mitter/Lodovico Scarfiotti and Vic Elford/Jochen Neerpasch. Paul Hawkins and David Hobbs captured another Gulf GT40 success at Monza, where the debutante 908 Coupés were fast but unreliable. Wyer did not bother to contest the Targa Florio, seeing this as Porsche territory, and Vic Elford drove a blinding race, aided by Umberto Maglioli in the works 907, after being delayed in the mountains by a flat tyre. Behind them were a pair of Alfa T33s, which had looked like winners when Elford was delayed.

The Porsche 908 took its first victory in the Nürburgring 1,000 Km, Jo Siffert and Vic Elford leading the sister model of Jo Siffert and Hans Herrmann. Ickx and Hawkins were close behind in third place, Wyer somewhat disappointed with his Australian driver's perform-

Pedro Rodriguez gives the thumbs-up as the Ford GT40 shared with Lucien Bianchi heads for the finishing line in 1968. The following year the same car won again, but by a much narrower margin (Ford).

ance that day. The Gulf Fords were victorious at Spa (Ickx and Redman) and again at Watkins Glen (Ickx and Lucien Bianchi), before Siffert won the half-distance, half-points race at the Zeltweg airfield in Austria.

Delaying the Le Mans 24-Hours until September was unfortunate for Wyer, since Brian Redman broke his arm while competing in the Belgian Grand Prix and Jacky Ickx broke his leg in a crash in Canada. His revised three-car team included Pedro Rodriguez and Lucien Bianchi, Brian Muir and Jackie Oliver and David Hobbs/Paul Hawkins, facing a quartet of Porsche 908 longtail coupés.

Porsche had not yet achieved good reliability with the 908s. Siffert and Herrmann led for three hours before retiring with a broken gearbox casing, two more went out with alternator failures and the Stommelen/Neerpasch 908 was delayed for an hour with a broken alternator, which was stripped and rebuilt in the pits, recovering to third place at the end.

Rodriguez made a steady start, reaching tenth position after the first hour, then moving up steadily. He and Bianchi took the lead at nightfall, a wet and miserable interlude. The main challenge came from an unexpected quarter, the Matra 630 powered by the state-financed V12 engine. Henri Pescarolo and Johnny Servoz-Gavin seemed to be well on course for a fine second place when two separate punctures put Pescarolo out of the contest with less than four hours remaining. Gratefully, Dieter Spoerry and Rico Steinemann inherited second in their privately–entered but works–prepared Porsche 907, delayed only by a cracked brake disc.

Two litre Alfa Romeo 33s occupied fourth, fifth and sixth places honourably, and the only Ferrari to be classified was in seventh place, the 275 LM driven by David Piper and Richard Attwood. In formation behind it were four Alpine-Renaults, well off the pace.

At the request of the organizers Ford had sponsored a new chicane before the pits, substantially reducing the speeds past the still unprotected working areas. Rolf Stommelen established a lap record at 3 min 38.1 sec, comparable with Phil Hill's 7 litre Ford record established in 1965 but vastly slower than Andretti's.

As a result of their success JW Automotive, Ford and Gulf collected the World Sports Car Championship, to everyone's surprise. Porsche had amassed more points but the best five scores would be decisive: the GT40 had won five of the ten races, Porsche the other five . . . but the Zeltweg race carried half points, so the title was lost.

The German company, though, had a secret weapon, one that would change the face of the championship. The FIA's attitude towards large capacity sports cars usually ran contrary to public opinion: spectators had loved the contest between the Ferrari 'P' cars, Ford's J cars and the Chaparrals, but the FIA banned them. The 5 litre stock-block Sports Prototypes, typified by the aging GT40 and Lola T70, were acceptable, and with some prodding from German

Only one Ford GT40 finished in '68, but one is enough to secure victory. Further back is the Hawkins/Hobbs entry which the Australian put into a sandbank, and ruined the clutch while getting out (Ford).

delegates the Parisian rulers decided to lower the 'homologation' ruling from 50 to 25 cars constructed, perhaps to encourage constructors like Lola and Chevron to produce more customer designs. The FIA played straight into Porsche's hands, and would soon regret their decision!

In Stuttgart Ferdinand Piëch and his team worked hard through the winter to produce the Porsche type 917, which astonished visitors to the Geneva Show in March 1969. The 908's flat-eight engine was enlarged, with four more cylinders, to become a flat-12 with a capacity of 4.4 litres and a power output of 520 bhp. This was installed in an adapted 907 type alloy spaceframe chassis and clothed with aerodynamic, 907 resembling coupé bodywork. Once developed it would render the GT40s and Lola T70s completely obsolete, but it would be a year before the Porsche 917 became a predictable winner.

Ferrari returned to the contest with the 312P model, effectively with the 420 bhp Formula 1 V12 engine in a two-seater formula car, and Pedro Rodriguez joined Chris Amon in the team's number one car. Lucien Bianchi, a true Belgian gentleman, joined the Autodelta Alfa Romeo team but was tragically killed when his T33 shed its rear bodywork during the Le Mans practice session, an accident that saddened everyone and caused Chiti to withdraw his team.

In the season's early races, Porsche's 908 was the model to beat without question, and the German company had already secured the

The Porsche 917 made its 24-Hour debut in 1969, and Vic Elford/Richard Attwood were leading by miles when their clutch bellhousing cracked on Sunday morning (Porsche).

1969 championship even before it arrived at Le Mans. For the 24-hour race Porsche entered three 908s and a pair of new 917s, cars which had already earned a reputation of being supremely difficult to drive. Moving flaps connected to the rear suspension marginally improved their stability on the Mulsanne Straight, where they reached 230 mph (370 km/h), but the FIA had already banned such devices in the wake of Formula 1 wing failures. The ACO had no alternative but to reject the moving flaps at scrutineering, at which Porsche's team manager Rico Steinemann threatened to withdraw all five cars from the race. Stalemate! Rolf Stommelen, Porsche's charger, was sent out in practice for observed laps, first with the flaps connected, then disconnected, and even the brave Vic Elford admitted to being impressed as Stommelen passed him at full speed. The FIA and the ACO stewards huddled, and allowed the flaps to be connected, but only for that race.

In John Wyer's cars were Jacky Ickx with Jackie Oliver, and David Hobbs with Mike Hailwood, their speed for the race precisely predetermined. Ickx, in fact, *walked* across the track at the start and fastened his seat belts with deliberation, advertising the team's aim of letting the Porsches and Ferraris get on with their race. This was, it proved, the last of the famous running starts, for in 1970 the pits would be protected by guardrail and, like all the other races, the 24-Hours would be started by a pace car.

Ickx's personal protest was justified, since John Woolfe, Porsche's

Hans Herrmann and Gérard Larrousse came within 70 metres of giving Porsche its first Le Mans victory in 1969, driving the 3 litre 908 model (Porsche).

first customer for the 917 model, crashed fatally at the White House on the opening lap, underlining just how difficult initially those cars were to drive. Chris Amon's Ferrari ran over the severed fuel tank and caught fire, and the track was virtually blocked. Rolf Stommelen and Vic Elford were the early pace-setters in their 917s followed, at some distance, by Siffert and Mitter in their Porsche 908s, and then Jo Bonnier in a Lola Chevrolet.

Stommelen's car was soon in trouble with an oil leak, and was later put out by a slipping clutch. Siffert/Redman took the lead, only to have their gearbox overheat and fail early in the evening. The new longtail bodywork shrouded the transmission too effectively.

Elford and Attwood led with ease throughout the night, nursing their 917's weak transmission with all possible care. Hans Herrmann and Gérard Larrousse lost 20 minutes when their 908 broke a wheel bearing (a common failure the previous season), and Udo Schutz crashed his 908 mightily at the Mulsanne kink, without coming to any harm.

On Sunday morning the 917 led the Rudi Lins/Willi Kauhsen 908, with Ickx and Oliver in third place and Herrmann/Larrousse fourth. It still looked good for Porsche, but in the pits there was growing anxiety as the 917's clutch slipped more and more. At midday the car was simply incapable of leaving the pits, although the drivers declared that they would have carried it round for the last four hours, if allowed. Almost simultaneously the Lins/Kauhsen 908 went out

The closest finish between rival makes was seen in 1969 after Jacky Ickx (Gulf Ford GT40) and Hans Herrmann (Porsche 908) passed and repassed for the final two hours. Herrmann's car was so close at the end . . . (Ford).

with a broken differential, and the last four hours of the race turned into a Grand Prix between Ickx/Oliver and Herrmann/Larrousse.

No motor racing film, John Frankenheimer's included, could have staged a better finish. For the last two hours Ickx and Herrmann passed and repassed. Ickx was simply brilliant in the heavy GT40, while the veteran Herrmann was more circumspect as his brake pad warning light was glowing. There was no time to change the pads, of course, and time and again Ickx outbraked him at the Mulsanne corner and led through Indianapolis, Arnage and White House to the finishing line. Herrmann's warning light was an electrical fault, though he didn't know it, and Ickx's car was due to refuel one lap before the four o'clock finish, but caution was thrown to the wind. The flag was shown, then Ickx came into sight from White House leading the white Porsche by 75 metres, the closest finish in the event's history between two rival makes.

The 1960s decade ended dramatically, but that was the last World Championship success for the GT40. Porsche's 908s filled the top three positions at Watkins Glen and then, in the last race of the year on the new Österreichring circuit, Jo Siffert and Kurt Ahrens gave the 917 its first victory . . .

Chapter 6

The French renaissance

THE 1970s started with a bang and went out with a whimper . . . Porsches dominated in 1970 and 1971 with the 917 model, followed by a marvellous era in which Matra collected a hat-trick of victories, and the series was then enlivened by a heady duel between the turbocharged sports cars of Porsche and Renault-Alpine. In the end, though, the Porsche factory exhausted itself and a privately–entered 935 Turbo won the 1979 race, a wet affair that pleased few people outside the Kremer Porsche team. The 1970s were rather low-key once the 5 litre models were outlawed, and the Middle East crisis contributed to a midway depression.

Ferrari's season with the 312P in 1969 had not brought any luck, and the announcement of the 917 had surprised him as much as everyone else. However, the Italian was in a position to do something about it, and Mauro Forghieri prepared the 5 litre, 12–cylinder 512 model for battle. The faithful Lampredi V12 engine was enlarged again to full 5 litre capacity and developed 570 bhp initially. Porsche developed their flat-12 to 4.9 litres and 600 horsepower, although most of the Le Mans entries ran at 4.5 litres to be on the safe side mechanically.

John Wyer had been invited to run the Porsche factory cars with Gulf sponsorship, the highest compliment he could imagine, and chief engineer John Horsman had found a substantial gain in downforce, and drivability, by shortening and raising the tail section. The 'Kurz' version was soon dominant in the 1,000 km races, but Porsche's own 'Langheck' (long tail) streamliner was faster at Le Mans. To Wyer's disgust, his own effort backed by the racing department was supplemented by two semi-official teams supplied by the customer department, one being Porsche Salzburg, the other run by Hans-Dieter Dechent and sponsored by Martini & Rossi. The Salzburg connection was a strong one, Porsche's distribution in Austria being headed by Ferry Porsche's sister, Louise Piëch, mother of Ferdinand who headed the 917 design team.

Seven Porsche 917s took the start ranged against 11 Ferrari 512S models, the Italian cars 80 kg (176 lb) heavier but considerably more powerful than all but the 4.9 litre Gulf-Porsches of Jo Siffert/Brian Redman and Pedro Rodriguez/Leo Kinnunen, and the Salzburg entry of Vic Elford/Kurt Ahrens. Wyer and Horsman had declined to use the factory's long tails, which proved to be a wise decision. Rain fell for most of the time, and the adapted short tail had a more aerodynamic form which proved nearly as fast, but easier to drive.

The Gulf-Porsches had a miserable race as it turned out. Rodriguez and Siffert chased Elford for the first hour, and Nino Vaccarella's Ferrari, the fastest of the Italian cars, retired with a broken connecting rod. Then Rodriguez retired with a broken distributor drive, and when rain set in at seven o'clock the contest was decimated, four of the Ferraris retiring in one mighty incident. Reine Wisell slowed, apparently trying to see through his smeared windscreen, and moments later Clay Regazzoni and Mike Parkes,

Another wet race, but Porsche's spirits weren't dampened as Hans Herrmann and Richard Attwood gave the 917 model, entered by Porsche Salzburg, its first Le Mans success, in 1970 (Porsche).

John Wyer's team, so successful with Fords, could not capture a victory with Porsche at Le Mans. The Siffert/Redman car failed in the night with engine trouble, when it was leading (Porsche).

followed by Derek Bell, became involved in a multiple accident. Wisell and Regazzoni were out immediately, Parkes limped his car back to the pits with heavy damage while Bell, whose car was unmarked, retired with engine failure.

Mike Hailwood decided to cover another lap before stopping for a change of tyres, and spun into the banking at the Dunlop Curve. That left Wyer with just the car driven by Siffert and Redman, and they led the race until 2 am when the Swiss driver missed a gear and over-revved the engine. Jacky Ickx spun his Ferrari at the Ford chicane in the night, sadly killing a marshal who was relaxing behind the armco, and all that was left of the race then was a duel between Attwood/Herrmann and Elford/Ahrens, both crews in Porsche Salzburg entries. Elford's luck was out again, his car retiring on Sunday with valve damage, so Hans Herrmann scored a popular victory that made up for defeat the year before. Then he announced his retirement from racing.

Gérard Larrousse and Willi Kauhsen finished second for the Martini team, Rudi Lins and Helmuth Marko third in their privately-entered 908, followed at a great distance by two privately-entered Ferrari 512s. Only seven cars finished that year, another nine — six of them Porsche 911s — excluded under the distance regulation after a horribly wet run.

Only seven cars finished the race in 1970, in awful weather conditions, and five of them were Porsches. This 'tail-end Charlie' was the 914/6 driven by Guy Chasseuil and Claude Ballot-Lena (Porsche).

The JW Gulf-Porsche team won seven of the season's ten championship races, but not the one that mattered most. Would it do better in 1971? It was, again, the dominant team with full 5 litre engines now developing 620 horsepower, while Ferrari had lightened the 512, now called the 512M, and claimed 630 bhp. The 5 litre Ferraris passed into private hands, though, as Ferrari lost interest. By this time the FIA had decided to ban the 5 litre cars — history repeating itself — and announced a 3 litre limit for 1972. That encouraged Ferrari to prepare a completely new 3 litre sports car around a flat-12 engine, the 312P/B. It was considerably more effective than the previous V12 design of 1969 and would win a lot of races. In 1971 though it was merely a thorn in Porsche's side, as was the Autodelta team's 3 litre tipo 33 model.

A Porsche victory at Le Mans was a foregone conclusion, eight privately-entered Ferrari 512Ms squaring up to seven works-supported Porsche 917s. The Ferrari factory kept well away, as did Autodelta after springing a major success at Brands Hatch. There was only one Matra MS660 for Chris Amon/Jean-Pierre Beltoise who failed to last the distance, retiring from an excellent third position on Sunday morning when the fuel pressure failed.

Pedro Rodriguez lowered the qualifying record to 3 min 13.9 sec, and with Jackie Oliver kept the race well under control until half

Opposite top *After a 21-year drought, French cars were winning again in the 1970s. The Matra-Simca team was victorious in 1972, '73 and '74, and each time Henri Pescarolo was the winner. Gérard Larrousse is the driver in this 1973 picture of the V12 powered 670B* (Autosport).

Opposite bottom *Three years of increasing effort paid off for Renault-Alpine, the French team conquering the 24-Hour event in 1978. Drivers of the A442 were Didier Pironi and Jean-Pierre Jaussaud* (Renault).

Below *Alfa Romeo increased its challenge in 1972 when the 5 litre cars were banished, but Andrea de Adamich (pictured) and Nino Vaccarella were well beaten in their Tipo 33 by the Matra team* (Alfa Romeo).

distance, but Jo Siffert and Derek Bell lost 70 minutes at nightfall having a broken shock absorber and damaged upright changed. Elford and Larrousse had retired the Martini entry when their cooling fan detached itself and went into orbit. Then during the night Gulf's third car driven by Attwood and Herbert Müller lost 40 minutes having the gearbox repaired.

The JW Automotive effort again seemed to be falling apart as Rodriguez stopped to have a seized hub upright changed. At half-distance the race was led by the Escuderia Montjuich Ferrari of José Juncadella and Nino Vaccarella, chased by the Martini team's 917 driven by Helmuth Marko and Gijs van Lennep, and then the three Gulf cars. Juncadella's Ferrari retired with a broken gearbox, but was followed into retirement on Sunday morning by Rodriguez with a split oil pipe which caused engine damage, and by Siffert with a split gearbox casing.

The race to the flag was won by Marko and van Lennep, little more than a lap ahead of Attwood/Müller, and theirs were the only 'big Porsches' to finish, many laps ahead of a trio of Ferrari 512Ms. Seven of the 13 cars classified were Porsche 911s, a sign of the times, and Porsche provided ten of the finishers.

Jaguar's build-up began in 1985 when Bob Tullius entered a pair of Group 44 team XJR-5 models. The shrill V12 engine excited the crowds, and Tullius won the IMSA GTP category.

The Silk Cut Jaguar team seemed to have a real chance of success in 1987 and at dawn on Sunday Martin Brundle and John Nielsen were going well in their XJR-8LM. Disappointment was around the corner (Jaguar).

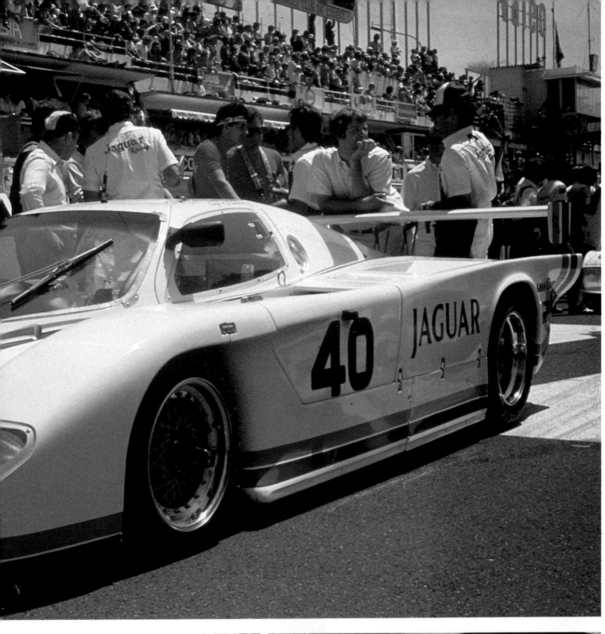

Five times winner Derek Bell is impressed as his Bognor neighbour John Watson tells a fishy story. Cigarette companies were well to the fore in the 1980s!

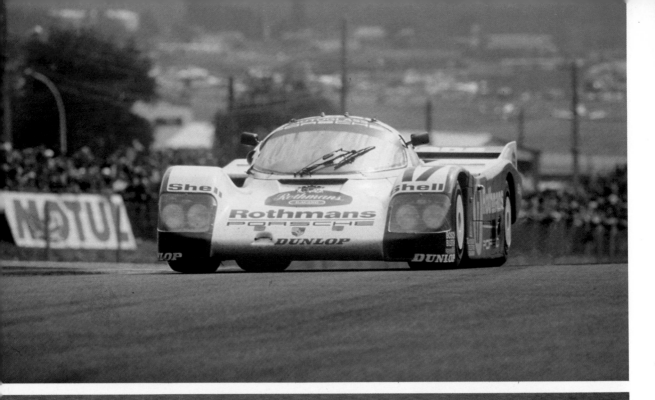

The 917's career ended sadly when its two major performers, Pedro Rodriguez and Jo Siffert, were killed within a few weeks of each other, the Mexican at the Norisring in Müller's Ferrari and the Swiss in a BRM at Brands Hatch. Memories of their personal duels in evenly matched Gulf-Porsches and as team-mates with BRM live on. With the advent of the 3 litre limitation in 1972, and the 650 kg (1,430 lb) minimum weight limit, Porsche chose to cross the Atlantic and dominate the Can-Am scene for a couple of years, developing the turbocharging technique.

For 1972 Ferrari prepared three superbly presented, totally competitive 312PB models for Jacky Ickx/Clay Regazzoni, Ronnie Peterson/Tim Schenken and Carlos Pace/Arturo Merzario, and they commanded the World Sports Car Championship even more effectively than Porsche had in the two previous years. In fact they won 10 out of 11 races, even taking the top four positions at the Österreichring when another car was prepared for Helmuth Marko, making Carlo Chiti's Autodelta Alfa Romeo T33/3 team look rather second-class. John Wyer engaged Derek Bell as his lead driver in the Gulf-Mirage team, using Ford Cosworth DFV engines in new Len Bailey–designed chassis, but would not attend Le Mans as he thought the engines to be unsuitable. Ferrari, too, had his doubts and withdrew his four-car team from the race, despite having set the fastest time in the April trials. An extended test at Monza had revealed transmission weaknesses, and the Matra-Simca team (a misnomer, since the V12 engines were developed by Matra's Georges Martin) started as the firm favourite. Against them were the Autodelta Alfas, a pair of Lola Ford DFVs, and Reinhold Joest's factory-loaned Porsche 908 Coupé, which could not be overlooked.

Jean-Pierre Beltoise, to share his Matra with Chris Amon, passed the startline on lap one several seconds ahead of his team-mates, only to have a connecting rod break as he lifted momentarily for the Dunlop Curve. The shrill V12 wail was replaced by a muffled explosion as the engine burst asunder and caught fire! One down, three to go.

The other French team cars were almost perfectly reliable, Henri Pescarolo and Graham Hill running in convoy with François Cevert and Howden Ganley for most of the way in first and second positions. Jean-Pierre Jabouille and David Hobbs made up places to run third at half distance, after early fuel pressure problems, only to break their gearbox in the last hour and spoil a 1-2-3 finish.

The race had been marred by Jo Bonnier's fatal accident, his Lola-Ford hitting the back of a Ferrari Daytona on Sunday morning and being launched into the trees at the Arnage turn. The Lolas had been quick while they lasted, Hughes de Fierlandt having led the first hourly bulletin, and in Bonnier's car Gijs van Lennep had established a new lap record at 3 min 46.9 sec. The circuit now included a new 'White House bypass' sponsored by Porsche, and called the Porsche Curves.

Graham Hill now achieved a unique record: twice World Champion in Formula 1, Indianapolis winner in 1966 and Le Mans winner in 1972. Cevert and Ganley might have finished closer in second place, but for a rainstorm on Sunday afternoon. Ganley slowed right down, taking extra care on wide tyres, and Marie-Claude Beaumont, the only lady driver in the race, ran into the back of the Matra with her Chevrolet Corvette. Surprisingly the Corvette retired, while the Matra was delayed only nine minutes having a new tail cover fitted. Third was Joest's Porsche 908 leading the de Adamich/Vaccarella Alfa Romeo, then five Ferrari Daytona 365 GTB/4 Grand Touring cars.

Matra and Ferrari enjoyed full-commitment combat throughout the 1973 season, and the previously supreme Italian cars were beginning to look rather ragged on occasions, especially in handling. The wheelbase was lengthened mid-season but it made little difference, and honours were being shared equally. Matra also had problems, in the engine department, but designer Martin found the cure in time for Le Mans by improving the lubrication system. For the 24-hour race there were four Matra V12s versus three Ferrari flat-12s, with Wyer's two Gulf-Mirages playing a strong supporting role. The Matras were made more reliable in MS670B form with new Porsche

The Matra V12 engined French sports cars were victorious in 1972, '73 and '74, their piercing noise leaving an indelible memory. Jean-Pierre Jabouille drives the MS 670B model to third place in 1973 (ACO).

designed gearboxes, and the fourth car was a back-up MS660 for Patrick Depailler/Bob Wollek with Hewland transmission.

A furious pace was set from the start, Arturo Merzario (Ferrari) and Jean-Pierre Beltoise (Matra) pulling away rapidly from their team-mates, but both runs seemed to be self-defeating. In the third hour Merzario's car was delayed by a split fuel collector pot, and was later delayed when the brake pad backing plates were almost welded to the discs (those of Redman and Ickx, who were called in for a check-up, were hardly bedded-in). Matra then ran into difficulties with their Goodyear tyres, which started chunking and delaminating, and both Beltoise/Cevert and Jabouille/Jaussaud were seriously delayed. To cap it all, the Depailler/Wollek Matra which had seen the lead briefly lost oil pressure and retired with a damaged engine.

In a race of predictable attrition, Beltoise's Matra crashed in the night after another tyre failure, and Carlos Reutemann retired his Ferrari from the lead with a blown engine. Ickx and Redman now moved smoothly into the lead chased by Pescarolo and Larrousse, while Carlo Facetti/'Pam'/Teo Zeccoli lay third in their Autodelta Alfa heading Jabouille and Jaussaud. JWA's Gulf team was out of the reckoning, the Hailwood/Watson/Schuppan Mirage retiring with accident damage — the young Australian had been told sternly to 'take it

Henri Pescarolo won three times in succession driving for Matra-Simca, the first time with Graham Hill then twice with Gérard Larrousse (Autosport).

easy, keep it in one piece' when lying fourth overall, and entered Tertre Rouge in a higher gear than may have been prudent, sliding gracefully into the ditch. Bell and Ganley, delayed by a gearbox rebuild, retired on Sunday morning with a broken oil pump.

The Ickx/Redman Ferrari succumbed gradually, losing its lead when a fractured exhaust pipe had to be changed, falling back again with a split fuel collector pot, and finally expiring with engine malaise less than two hours from the finish. Pescarolo and Larrousse eased off to finish six laps ahead of the Merzario/Pace Ferrari, while third was the remaining Matra of the two Jean-Pierres, Jabouille and Jaussaud. Fourth was the much-modified works Porsche 911 Carrera RSR driven by Gijs van Lennep and Herbert Müller, fourth a privately-entered Porsche 908 and fifth the GT class winning Ferrari Daytona of Vic Elford and Claude Ballot-Lena. It had been an epic race.

The 1974 season held no such surprises, for Ferrari pulled out of sports car racing completely to concentrate better on Formula 1 — and to make Niki Lauda into a champion — leaving the field open to Matra, Alfa Romeo and Gulf-Mirage.

The Matra-Simca team, managed by chassis designer Gerard Ducarouge, really had nothing to fear but itself . . . engine failures sidelined both cars in the opening round at Monza, letting the Autodelta Alfa Romeos into a popular 1-2-3 placing. That, however, was a temporary lapse on Matra's part, and the French went on to win the next nine races in succession, including Le Mans.

Alfa Romeo was looking increasingly disorganized and withdrew from that race, which seemed to belong to Matra despite opposition from two Gulf-Mirages and a pair of turbocharged, factory Porsche 911 Carreras. It was a race that Matra could not afford to lose, yet for much of the time the issue was in some doubt.

Early in the race Jean-Pierre Jarier collided with a Porsche 911 in the absurdly crowded pits lane, dropping right down the order as the damage was repaired, and Jabouille's Matra was overheating badly almost from the start.

During the evening the Reine Wisell/Vern Schuppan Gulf-Mirage retired with a broken driveshaft, and the Bell/Hailwood Gulf-Mirage lost time as grease was pouring from the driveshaft constant velocity joints. The Helmuth Koinigg/Manfred Schurti Porsche Carrera Turbo blew up spectacularly on the Mulsanne Straight, and at midnight the leading Matras of Jaussaud/Wollek and Beltoise/Jarier retired, almost at the same time, with connecting rod failures.

Pescarolo and Larrousse, leading, could only cross their fingers and hope for the best, but on Sunday morning Pescarolo stopped at Mulsanne with a broken gearbox. He returned slowly to the pits for a rebuild, which took an hour, but was still able to drive away with a lap in hand over the Porsche Turbo of van Lennep and Müller. Then

Porsche developed the turbocharged 911 model for the 1974 season, and Müller/van Lennep brought theirs home second behind the Matra. Illustrated is the Manfred Schurti/Helmuth Koinigg car which retired (Porsche).

It was Larrousse who crossed the finishing line in the winning Matra in 1974, completing the famous French hat-trick (Haymarket).

they, too, had a gearbox failure, losing third and fifth ratios, but they elected to carry on at reduced speed to finish in second place, still ahead of the overheating Matra of Jabouille and Migault, and the Bell/Hailwood Gulf-Mirage. It had not been a classic race, but there was plenty of activity in the pits.

The hat-trick for Matra-Simca, and for Henri Pescarolo, had certainly brought France to the forefront in sports car racing, but the world was then grappling with fuel shortages and soaring prices. Motor races and rallies were being cancelled on a large scale, and in America the Can-Am series was restricted on fuel to the extent that Porsche lost interest. It was cancelled completely in 1975. Simca withdrew support from Matra, leading the aerospace company to pull out of the sports car formula, and the Automobile Club de l'Ouest announced that the 1975 edition of the 24-Hours race would have new regulations, based on fuel economy, limiting the size of the fuel tanks and enforcing a minimum of 20 laps between each refuelling stop.

Fuel economy would have to be improved by at least 25 per cent, and only the Cosworth DFV in detuned form could possibly meet the target. Renault and Alpine, developing a turbocharged version of the 2 litre V6 racing engine, abandoned ideas of participating, as did the Alfa Romeo team which had now been sold off to the German

*Another change in regulations, in 1975, put the accent on fuel economy. John Wyer's Gulf-Mirage team had the answer, with the Ford-Cosworth V8 powered GR8, and Jacky Ickx/ Derek Bell were the successful drivers. Talking to Bell is team engineer John Horsman (*Moto-foto*).*

entrant, Willibert Kauhsen, and was doing rather well in the emasculated sportscar championship.

Essentially, the race was between two Gulf-Mirage GR8 DFV models driven by Derek Bell/Jacky Ickx and Vern Schuppan/Jean-Pierre Jaussaud, with engines detuned rather conservatively to 370 bhp, two heavier Ligier JS2 coupés with their DFV engines developing 420 bhp, two Lola DFVs and four elderly Porsche 908s.

The race was not part of the World Sports Car Championship on account of its unique regulations, and the spectators stayed away in their thousands as Bell and Ickx led almost from start to finish, delayed only by a broken exhaust pipe on Sunday afternoon. The lapse allowed the Ligier driven by Jean-Louis Lafosse and Guy Chasseuil to draw close, but the Frenchmen had to settle for second place ahead of the Mirage driven by Schuppan and Jaussaud. It was not, by any stretch of imagination, a vintage year at Le Mans, but it provided a second success for Ickx and got Bell off the mark.

New regulations were introduced in 1976 introducing two fresh breeds of cars; Group 5 'silhouette' models based on production cars competing for the World Championship for Manufacturers, and Group 6 'prototypes' competing for the World Sports Car Championship. The FIA decreed that the two championships would not overlap but the ACO, making a wise decision, remained outside the

New regulations in 1976 brought Porsche right back into the frame with turbocharged cars, the 936 starting a brilliant Le Mans career by winning in the hands of Jacky Ickx and Gijs van Lennep (Porsche).

regulations by combining the two series for the 24-Hour race, at the same time abandoning the fuel consumption restrictions.

Porsche had prepared cars for both major series, the 911 Turbo based 935 and the 936 prototype, both powered by turbocharged flat-six production-based engines. Jacky Ickx and Jochen Mass contested both championships for the factory, and there were also Grand Touring class 934 models, again based on the 911 Turbo, for customers. Porsche won all three classes in 1976.

Renault was to build up its effort gradually, starting only one A442 model for Jabouille and Patrick Tambay in 1976. The Porsche 936s of Ickx/van Lennep and Jürgen Barth/Reinhold Joest were well in control throughout the night, the Renault having been delayed by an electrical fault and high engine temperature. Barth's Porsche expired on Sunday morning with a broken driveshaft while Ickx continued to take his third victory, delayed only by a broken exhaust pipe which lowered the turbocharging pressure. At the finish it had 11 laps in hand over the Harley Cluxton–owned Mirage-Ford of Lafosse and Migault, while in third place was the privateer Lola-DFV effort of Alain de Cadenet and Chris Craft. The Porsche 935 of Rolf Stommelen and Manfred Schurti was competitive too, claiming fourth ahead of Bell and Schuppan in the second Mirage-Ford.

There were two halcyon years ahead for the 24-Hour race as Renault and Porsche continued their battle, almost to the exclusion of other makes. The French marque had vowed to win the race but

Porsche was determined too, and its greater experience was an asset. Four Renault-Alpines, all with 520 bhp V6 turbo engines, were backed by two Renault–engined Mirages, and on paper Renault held a major advantage over Porsche, with just two twin-turbo 936s which developed 540 bhp.

Reliability would be the key, and such was the pace in 1977 that few of the turbo cars would finish. More than anything turbo-related failures such as piston breakages would contribute to the attrition, although Porsche's effort was reduced by 50 per cent early on when a connecting rod broke in the engine powering Ickx and Pescarolo. The Belgian was switched to the second car, sharing with Jürgen Barth and Hurley Haywood, already delayed by a fuel injection pump breakage and in forty-first place half an hour behind.

Ickx drove another of his inspired races, constantly under the lap record during the night and passing the two Mirage-Renaults. The V6 engines were not too reliable and on Sunday morning the Porsche was up to second place, six laps behind the Renault of Jabouille and Bell . . . until that car blew a piston. As the Porsche led for the first time, the last remaining Renault of Patrick Depailler and Jacques Laffite expired with a broken piston, and dramas continued to the end, Ickx's Porsche also breaking a piston 45 minutes before the finish.

Porsche's 936 won again in 1977, Ickx partnered this time with Hurley Haywood and Jürgen Barth. An epic drive vanquished the Renaults, but the Porsche finished on five cylinders (Porsche).

Above *Renault mounted a huge effort in 1977, entering four Renault-Alpine A442 sports cars with turbocharged V6 engines. They overwhelmed the Porsches at first, but none reached the finish (Renault).*

Opposite top *The most striking car in the 1978 race was the Martini Porsche 935/78 driven by Rolf Stommelen and Manfred Schurti. The new 3.2 litre, 24-valve engine developed 750 bhp and the 935 was as fast as the Group 6 entries, but a troubled run dropped it to eighth place (Porsche).*

Opposite bottom *Backing the Renault team in 1977 was a pair of Mirage-Renaults entered by the American, Harley Cluxton. This one driven by Sam Posey and Michel Leclère failed to finish, but Vern Schuppan and Jean-Pierre Jarier saved face for the French manufacturer by finishing second (Renault).*

Such was its lead over the Mirage-Renault of Schuppan and Jarier that the Porsche could not be overtaken, so the German team removed the spark plug and Barth made two slow laps at the end to qualify safely. A lot of engines needed rebuilding in the days that followed, but Porsche — and Ickx — had now notched up a fourth Le Mans victory.

Alfa Romeo had the only team worth mentioning in the World Sports Car Championship that year, but abstained from Le Mans, and the Group 6 championship was then summarily cancelled by the FIA. Porsche's domination of the World Championship for Manufacturers was absolute, although the factory left most of the running to customer teams — those of the Kremer brothers, Reinhold Joest, Georg Loos and Max Moritz — and on its own account developed four-valve cylinder heads with water cooling for the official 935 and 936 entries.

One spectacular 935, the /78 model, was prepared to explore the limits of the Group 5 regulations. Ickx and Mass strode to victory at Silverstone in this 750 bhp monster, now taken out to 3.2 litres, and it was entrusted to Rolf Stommelen and Manfred Schurti for the 24-hour race. The main effort would concentrate on a pair of 936/78 sports cars, which now developed 580 bhp from 2.1 litres, backed by one two-valve car. This was the heaviest assault ever mustered by the German company, since the entries in 1970 and 1971 had been

Porsche's 'second string' cars at Le Mans were the Group 5 935 models. The Stommelen/Schurti entry retired but a similar car driven by Peter Gregg/Claude Ballot-Lena finished third (Porsche).

ostensibly handled by private teams with factory assistance.

Renault had put its cars through a rigorous development programme and carried out more than 30 modifications on the engines alone. The nationalized company again entered four cars, two A442s, an A442B and an A443, the latter with a 2.1 litre engine and a bubble canopy, backed up again by a pair of Harley Cluxton Mirage-Renaults.

As expected it was a marathon contest, and Porsche helped Renault's cause by making early pit stops to adjust the fuel pressure, Ickx/Pescarolo and Haywood/Gregg both being delayed. Jabouille and Depailler led, with Pironi/Jaussaud a lap behind after four hours, and

the Porsche of Wollek/Barth running strongly in third position.

Stommelen's 935/78, nick-named 'Moby Dick', misfired its way through the race and never showed its real potential, struggling to eighth place at the end, and Ickx's car was delayed 45 minutes by a breakage of fifth gear on Saturday evening. This was, and continued to be, the weakest part of the 936 design, and the Belgian was immediately switched to the Wollek/Barth car which, so far, had been trouble-free.

Jarier and Bell retired in the night with a broken transmission on their Renault, but Jabouille and Depailler looked untroubled in the lead, their Renault two laps ahead of Ickx. Then, for the second time in the race, Ickx was to lose time with a broken fifth gear. That was repaired in 40 minutes but then the leading Renault of Jabouille/Depailler went out with a broken piston.

As in 1977 the 24-hour race was becoming a battle of survivors, and Didier Pironi/Jean-Pierre Jaussaud did all that was required in bringing their Renault-Alpine A442B home five laps ahead of Wollek/Barth/Ickx, and seven laps ahead of Gregg/Haywood/Joest. This was a great victory for Renault, and one which would signal the end of the company's sports car activities. In future Formula 1 racing would be the priority.

Really the lights were turned off then. Porsche became increasingly remote, leaving all the running to its customers, and was only persuaded to enter two cars for the race in 1979 by David Thieme's Essex Petroleum company, with reluctance it seemed. This time there was no ongoing programme, and a warm-up for the 936 in the Silverstone 1,000 Km turned out badly when tyres turned on the rims, giving Brian Redman a bad fright and Jochen Mass a high-speed crash.

With little opposition, Porsche's factory team seemed dispirited at Le Mans in 1979, the minds of the engineers concentrating on the forthcoming Indianapolis 500 car design. The race started well, Ickx and Redman leading Wollek and Haywood, but then the Englishman had another tyre failure at the Dunlop Curve and lost time getting back to the pits. Worse, the flailing rubber had damaged the bodywork and cooling system, and the engine was never quite the same again. During the night the alternator belt sheared, and although Ickx restarted he was later disqualified for receiving outside assistance, in the form of a replacement belt.

Wollek and Haywood coped with a misfiring engine, which lost compression and expired on Sunday morning, and by that time most of the Cosworth entries had failed with transmission and engine failures. The closing stages developed into a contest between the Group 5 Porsche 935s, the Kremer K3 model driven by Klaus Ludwig and the American Whittington brothers, Don and Bill, and Dick Barbour's 935 driven by the American owner with Rolf Stommelen and film star Paul Newman.

In wet weather conditions the Kremer team lost nearly an hour

Renault's bid for victory finally succeeded in 1978 when Didier Pironi and Jean-Pierre Jaussaud convincingly beat the Porsche team. The winning car featured an unusual 'bubble top' which increased the maximum speed to 225 mph (Renault).

For the first time in postwar history a production–based car won the 24-Hour race in 1979, the Porsche 935 prepared by the Kremer brothers for Klaus Ludwig and the American brothers Don and Bill Whittington (Porsche).

when the fuel injection pump snapped, but still had enough cushion to beat Barbour's Porsche which was delayed by a jammed wheel nut. In third place, then, was an all-French crew in another Porsche 935 leading a Porsche 934 which claimed the GT prize.

This had not been a good demonstration of Group 6, but the decade had enjoyed some highlights: the power of the Porsche 917s and the Ferrari 512s, the ear-splitting performances of the Matra team, and the muffled tones of turbo Porsches and Renault-Alpines in action. But still, four French victories between 1972 and 1978 was a fine achievement for the nationalistic race to applaud, and Le Mans resident Jean Rondeau looked stronger each year with his own Group 6 chassis, albeit with Cosworth power.

Chapter 7

Porsche über alles

Porsche let the 1980 race go almost by default, but returned the following year with a turbocharged winner that presaged the most dominant display in the history of sports car racing, certainly so far as Le Mans was concerned. Even Ferrari's records were eclipsed as Porsche successes went on, and on, and on . . . there was nothing that Ford could do about it, nor Aston Martin, nor Mercedes, but Jaguar's attempts were becoming stronger each year and eventually toppled the German dynasty in 1988.

A rather strange decision was made in Stuttgart in 1979. Managing director Professor Ernst Fuhrmann stated that in 1980 Porsche would contest the race with a trio of Porsche 924 Carreras, 2 litre turbocharged models which developed 320 bhp at best. There was no likelihood of these winning, in fact the company would gladly settle for a place in the top six, but technical director Helmuth Bott did the decent thing and lent a factory 936 to Reinhold Joest, although it was a 'back door' arrangement and word was put out that Joest had built a replica. It was powered by a two-valve engine on low boost, but still developing 550 bhp; that should be more than enough to deal with the Cosworth contingent, with 450 bhp at most, and Jacky Ickx was tempted out of retirement to drive the car with Joest.

Jean Rondeau was the main contestant with three M379B models, with curvaceous bodywork and with engines finely tuned by the Swiss expert, Heini Mader. Rondeau drove one car himself, with '78 winner Jean-Pierre Jaussaud, the second was handled by Henri Pescarolo and Jean Ragnotti, the third by Gordon Spice and the Belgian Martin brothers, Jean-Michel and Philippe. Two WM-Peugeots were in the race, powered by production based, turbocharged V6 engines and they, like the strong Porsche 935 contingent, had outside chances of winning.

Porsche's 924 Carrera turbo model was the mainstay of the factory in 1980, rather controversially, and Jürgen Barth and Manfred Schurti did well to claim sixth place overall (Porsche).

The ACO had again devised some unique rules for the race. Fuel tanks were limited to 120 litres (26.4 gallons) and the rate of refuelling to one litre per second, so that each stop for a full tank would occupy two minutes. That in itself was a deterrent to the turbocharged cars, and there were more: the cars' qualifying times would be based on the average times of the two or three drivers (this led to tremendous rows after practice), and no components could be changed from the start of practice to the end of the race. If an engine was damaged on Thursday evening, it wouldn't start the race. 'All very French . . .' people said.

From the start, on a soaking track, Porsche 935s made the running, Bob Wollek handily placed in the Georg Loos entry, pursued by John Fitzpatrick in Barbour's car and Tetsu Ikuzawa in Kremer's.

Second overall in 1980 was the factory-loaned Porsche 936 prepared and driven by Reinhold Joest, shared with Jacky Ickx. A gearbox problem ruled out victory (Porsche).

As the track dried in the fourth hour Ickx and Joest moved ahead, and looked secure until a broken alternator belt stopped the unique Porsche on the Mulsanne Straight. This time there was a spare belt for Ickx to fit, but he lost 14 minutes and the lead passed to the Pescarolo/Ragnotti Rondeau.

A spate of piston failures sidelined the leading Porsche 935s during the night and they were joined in retirement by Pescarolo's Rondeau, with a blown head gasket. Then, on Sunday morning, the 936's weak-spot was revealed again as Joest's Group 6 car pulled up with a broken fifth gear, losing 25 minutes during the rebuild. Jean Rondeau and Jean-Pierre Jaussaud went ahead, but there was still more excitement to come.

A heavy rainstorm swept the course at lunchtime, and Rondeau spun the leading car helplessly at the Dunlop Curve, glancing off the armco and stalling in the middle of the track. He was missed by a spinning 2-litre entry, then missed again by Joest who aquaplaned past, and after an agonizing delay Rondeau managed to get the engine running and continued his way. Another downpour, shorter this time, in the last hour led Jaussaud to spin, but he kept going on slick tyres and, as Ickx stopped for wet weather tyres, the rain eased off.

Another French victory was in the bag, and never had success been more popular. The Le Mans resident constructor became the first to win the 24-hour race in a car bearing his own name, and he and Jaussaud were near to tears as the national anthem was played.

Ickx was second again, the Spice/Martin/Martin Rondeau was a good third followed by the Guy Frequelin/Roger Dorchy WM-Peugeot, and Jürgen Barth/Manfred Schurti/Eberhard Braun were sixth in the best of the Porsche 924 Carrera GTs. The other two, one of them driven by Derek Bell, were sorely afflicted by burned-out exhaust valves, finishing twelfth and thirteenth. It was not a marvellous outing for Bell, but it was his ticket to the Porsche factory team in the years to come.

On the first day of January 1981 Porsche appointed a new chief executive, Peter W. Schutz, whose approach to the running of the business, and to competitions, was more outgoing than Prof Fuhrmann's had been, and was more in tune with the ideas of Professor Porsche himself. One of the first decisions taken was to develop the 936 model and to bring it back to Le Mans, and at Weissach there was an ideal power unit collecting dust: the Indy project had turned sour, since USAC changed the rules in an arbitrary way, and the flat-six engine had been developed to 2.65 litre capacity. With some modifications to suit it to the task it developed 620 bhp with ease, and to cope with this power Porsche resurrected the old Can-Am four-speed transmission; the ratios were not ideal, but it was virtually indestructible with a rating to 1,000 horsepower.

Two cars were presented in June 1981 for Jacky Ickx/Derek Bell

Surely the most popular victory in the history of the race was achieved in 1980 by the Le Mans constructor Jean Rondeau, whose Ford-Cosworth V8 powered Rondeau shared with Jean-Pierre Jaussaud beat Joest and Ickx by two laps (Autosport).

and for Jochen Mass/Vern Schuppan/Hurley Haywood, and they were the class of the field, no doubt. In opposition were three Rondeaus, two of them powered by the latest 3.3 litre Cosworth DFL V8 engines but still nowhere near the Porsches on performance.

Ickx and Bell enjoyed a race that was perfect by any standards, losing not a minute in 24 hours in their 936 sponsored by Jules, a fragrance company. They were, as someone pointed out, smelling of roses, but Mass's luck was never good — he was the first visitor to the pits with a broken spark plug, lost more time with a broken clutch, and finished a very disappointing thirteenth after the mechanics had probed a fuel injection problem.

Jean-Louis Lafosse lost his life when his Rondeau left the road on the Mulsanne Straight, probably due to earlier body damage, and that put a blight on the constructor's challenge. Jean Rondeau talked to all his drivers before making the decision to continue, though not without further setbacks. Both the 3.3 litre models lost time with broken fuel pump drives, while the DFV–powered Rondeaus plugged on to second and third places: Jacques Haran/Jean-Louis Schlesser/Philippe Streiff were 14 laps behind the winning Porsche despite a gearbox problem, and Gordon Spice/François Migault were third after the ignition system had been repaired twice. Rondeau himself and Jaussaud retired in the night with serious handling problems.

Group C was a complete innovation in 1982, introducing a formula oriented to fuel consumption to the entire championship. It had been felt for a long time that the factories producing turbocharged engines, notably Porsche and Lancia at that time, could have as much power

One of the most perfect runs in the history of the race was recorded by the factory Porsche 936 in 1981, Jacky Ickx and Derek Bell losing no time and covering 2,999 miles, a record distance (Porsche).

as they wanted, though at great expense, and manufacturers such as Aston Martin, Jaguar and Ford would always face such a crippling disadvantage that they could never take part.

FISA, the FIA's sporting commission, announced a formula which restricted the manufacturers and teams to 600 litres for 1,000 km races, and pro rata for Le Mans, effectively limiting all types of engine to about 700 horsepower. Porsche never claimed more than 650 bhp for their engines and remained fully competitive, although later on Lancia, Jaguar, Mercedes and Nissan all claimed 700 bhp, even when the fuel allocation was reduced to 510 litres in 1985.

Several teams saw the Ford Cosworth V8 as being the ideal unit, and the 3.3 litre DFL version was increased in capacity to 3.9 litres for those who wanted it, the maximum power output rising to 550 bhp. It was hardly enough, and the engine was prone to serious vibration which tended to break ancillary parts. Designer Keith Duckworth planned a lightly turbocharged version for 1983, and even envisaged using counterbalance shafts, but the programme was halted before these developments could be tested.

There was a good variety of cars to be seen in 1982: Jean Rondeau produced the aerodynamic M482, Ford had Len Bailey design the C100 (so called because the maximum height at the top of the windscreen was 100 cm, recalling the GT40's 40 in height), Peter Sauber in Switzerland adapted a BMW-powered car to accept the DFL, and Eric Broadley of Lola designed the T600 for the V8 engine. In Germany, Reinhold Joest manufactured the Porsche 936C, based on the previous year's winner, and the Kremer brothers in Cologne produced the C-K5 also with Porsche's flat-six turbo engine.

There was also a 'Junior' class in 1983 with a lesser fuel allocation, of 320 litres for 1,000 km, and this would be much cheaper to contest since maximum power would be restricted to 400-450 bhp. The only serious contestant, initially, was the Italian Alba-Giannini team of pharmaceuticals millionaire Martino Finotto, whose co-driver Carlo Facetti designed the 1.8 litre turbocharged engine. Each engine had to emanate from a manufacturer with cars running in homologated categories, and the Giannini company 'endorsed' Finotto's design.

The Americans had decided not to support a consumption formula and devised separate regulations for the IMSA GTP category, although the cars were similar. The Daytona, Sebring and Watkins Glen races would not form part of the World Championship, reducing the 1982 series to eight rounds, and to make matters more complicated existing Group 5 and Group 6 designs were allowed to compete in the first year, to make up the numbers. Lancia therefore ran a very light and potent 1.4 litre turbocharged Group 6 car (which was a brand-new design!) in an effort to win the Drivers' Championship for Riccardo Patrese or Michele Alboreto, even though the team was not eligible for Constructors' points.

Henri Pescarolo and Giorgio Francia won the opening round of the new Group C season for Jean Rondeau, at Monza, taking their 3.9 DFL powered M382 to a fine victory over the Rolf Stommelen/Ted Field Porsche 935, and Patrese and Alboreto won the second round at Silverstone. The victory was qualified, because the Lancia was ineligible for championship points, and the real winner was the new Porsche 956 on its debut in the hands of Jacky Ickx and Derek Bell, desperately conserving fuel. Officialdom had overlooked the fact that Silverstone was traditionally a six-hour race, and in that time the Lancia covered 1,132 km (703 miles), a distance beyond the duration of the new Porsche at full speed on its fuel allocation!

Porsche and their new sponsors, Rothmans, had three cars at Le Mans and did not expect the fuel restriction to be a major handicap. The 956 model was the Stuttgart firm's first monocoque design, it had ground effects which increased cornering speeds, and was about to prove itself far superior to anything else on the circuits.

The three 956s driven by Ickx and Bell, Mass and Schuppan, and Haywood/Holbert/Barth droned round the course with the greatest precision, while one by one the Ford-Cosworth powered challengers fell by the wayside. Both the 3.9 litre Rondeaus stopped within minutes of each other with dead engines, the vibrations breaking the flywheel ignition sensors, and the two Ford C100s had also been put out by transmission and engine failures.

If it was a race of survival, the winners had to be Porsche. Joest's 936C, driven by Wollek and the Martin brothers, was the only machine that could remotely challenge the Rothmans team, and held a good third place when Holbert's car lost time — first a door flew off, then it had a wheel bearing failure. Shortly before the finish the Joest Porsche went out with an engine failure, and the factory team's

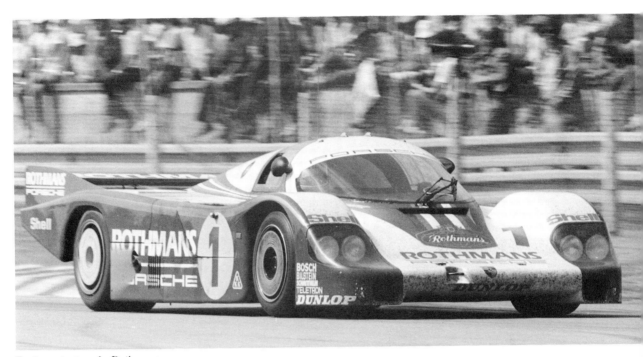

Factory prepared Rothmans-Porsche 956 models were first, second and third overall in 1982 on their début at the Sarthe, a crushing success. It was the Belgian driver's sixth victory, an all-time record (Porsche).

three cars formed up in triumphant number and race order, 1-2-3, for the finish.

Porsche 935s, those of John Fitzpatrick/David Hobbs and Dany Snobeck/François Servanin/François Migault, took fourth and fifth places, while a Ferrari 512BB was sixth.

An interesting car in seventh place was the Aston Martin Nimrod, powered by the Newport Pagnell company's 5.3 litre V8 engine and driven by Ray Mallock, Simon Phillips and Mike Salmon. Aston Martin dealer Robin Hamilton had arranged the building of two cars, with the chassis based on the Lola T70 and adapted by Eric Broadley for the task. It was absurdly heavy at 1,050 kg (2,310 lb), far more than the 800 kg (1,760 lb) minimum, but everyone applauded the effort.

Porsche's scoreboard was gaining now, with seven wins at Le Mans for the manufacturer, six for Ickx and three for Bell . . . but they weren't finished yet.

The 956 model ran out the winner at Spa, Fuji and Brands Hatch to take the Group C title, though only by a slender margin over Jean Rondeau's team which contested all the rounds qualifying for the Manufacturer's title and scored well in most of them. Jacky Ickx won the Drivers' championship, too, by the narrowest of margins after a hectic race at Brands Hatch, where he beat the Lancia of Riccardo Patrese and Teo Fabi by a superhuman effort, overtaking the nimbler car on aggregate to win by less than five seconds, in five and a half hours.

The Lancias had done their reputation no good at all at Le Mans, both cars retiring with electrical and fuel pump failure within 15 minutes of the start, but under Cesare Fiorio's direction they entered Group C properly in 1983 with the LC2 model, designed by Dallara and powered by a twin-turbo version of the Ferrari 2.65 litre V8 engine. On paper, at least, it was a superior car in every way, but three years of effort brought very little in the way of results, the Italian company always being more successful in the sphere of rallying.

Newly appointed to direct Ford's competitions programme, Stuart Turner summarily cancelled the ill-fated C100 design and all projects connected with it, including further development of the 3.9 litre DFL. The whole programme had been a shambles in 1982 and Turner would not allow it to be repeated, although the car was beginning to show promise and might have been reasonably successful in private hands.

No-one kidded themselves any more that Porsche had any real opposition, save from Lancia. The Cosworth engines lacked power and reliability, although later they would prove ideal, in 3.3 litre form, for the Junior class when re-coded C2. Porsche laid down a production line of 956 models for customers, prominent among these being Reinhold Joest (who straight away won the opening round of the 1983 season, at Monza), John Fitzpatrick (who, with Derek Warwick beat the works cars at Brands Hatch), Erwin Kremer, and Richard Lloyd with sponsorship from Canon.

Porsche's 956 model recorded the most comprehensive victory at Le Mans in 1983, taking the top eight places. Al Holbert, Vern Schuppan and Hurley Haywood beat team-mates Ickx and Bell by less than half a lap, and are jubilant on the ACO's balcony (Rothmans).

Eleven Porsche 956s started the 24-Hours race in 1983 and only two retired, those of Fitzpatrick with a fuel pump failure, and Mass whose engine gave up four hours from the finish. In the most convincing display of supremacy ever witnessed at Le Mans, Porsches claimed the top eight places and tenth! A BMW 6-cylinder powered Sauber was the only car to dent Porsche's armour, ever so slightly in ninth place, and the competition simply fell apart in trying.

Three Lancia Martinis failed to get on terms even in the opening stages and retired with a variety of mechanical problems. All three Rondeaus retired with breakages in their 3.9 litre DFL engines, a fact which signalled the end of that programme.

The race among Porsche drivers was a keen one, the three Rothmans cars always setting the pace until Mass's engine gradually turned sour on Sunday morning. Bell was delayed when the Motronic engine management system played up, going two laps behind the Holbert/Haywood/Schuppan car, and when that seemed to be the final order Holbert's left-side door blew away, spoiling the stream of cooling air to the radiator. The engine began to seize up on the last lap, while Bell threw himself at the task of passing, but the task was too great. The result was a grandstand finish, witnessed by Mario and Mike Andretti, with Philippe Alliot in Kremer's 956 which finished third.

FISA had intended to reduce the fuel allocation for C1 cars by 15

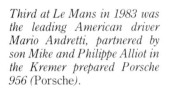

Third at Le Mans in 1983 was the leading American driver Mario Andretti, partnered by son Mike and Philippe Alliot in the Kremer prepared Porsche 956 (Porsche).

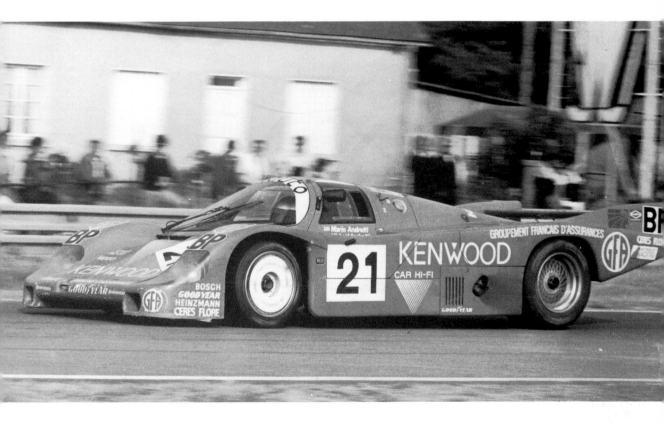

per cent in 1984, to 510 litres per 1,000 km, but after the IMSA Daytona 24-hour race in February it was announced that the reduction would be cancelled, possibly as a prelude to integrating the IMSA and Group C championship regulations. It was a vain hope, as it turned out, but the Porsche and Lancia factories reacted angrily having spent considerable sums of money on engine management development, Porsche with Bosch and the Motronic system and Lancia with Weber-Marelli.

On Porsche's behalf, competitions director Peter Falk withdrew the Rothmans team entries for Le Mans. Lancia might have been inclined to do the same, but pressure from the sponsors Martini & Rossi persuaded Cesare Fiorio to enter two works cars, LC2/84 models, in which the engines had been enlarged to 3.1 litres. The new engine capacity was not revealed until after the race, however.

Taking part in the 1984 event were 12 privately–entered Porsche 956s, two works Lancias and a privately–entered LC2/83, two Aston Martin Nimrods entered by Viscount Downe, and two Group 44 Jaguar XJR-5s from Bob Tullius's stable in America. Although Tullius was concentrating on the IMSA championship, and his cars were designed for that formula, he was fascinated by the challenge of Le Mans and was getting plenty of help and encouragement from the Jaguar factory in Coventry.

There were a couple of WM-Peugeots in the race too, and Roger Dorchy took it upon himself to be the 'hare' of the race, turning up the boost and leading the first lap. His heroism got out of hand at the end of the Mulsanne Straight on the second lap, and in braking too hard he half spun and just avoided having a major accident. He continued, only to repeat the manoeuvre on the third lap and wipe the nose off his car!

Bob Wollek and Sandro Nannini, in the quicker works Lancia, ran well through Saturday evening in company with a convoy of Porsche 956s, those of Joest, Kremer and the American entrant Preston Henn coming to the fore. At half distance the second Lancia driven by Paolo Barilla/Hans Heyer/Mauro Baldi broke fifth gear in its Hewland transmission and four hours later Wollek and Nannini suffered the same fate, which cost them the lead. Barilla's car retired on Sunday morning with a broken distributor drive, while Wollek's had further problems with its gearbox and finished eighth.

The two Aston Martin Nimrods were eliminated in one dreadful accident on Saturday evening, John Sheldon losing control of his car at the infamous Mulsanne 'kink' when a tyre deflated suddenly, due no doubt to a slow puncture. He hit the guardrails at great speed, almost 200 mph (320 km/h), and the Nimrod came to rest in the centre of the track burning fiercely. Team-mate Drake Olson hit some of the wreckage and was put out of the race, and a marshal lost his life.

The two Tullius Jaguars, with V12 engines, were being driven conservatively, lying sixth and seventh at half distance. Daylight

would bring no luck, for one car suffered a tyre failure and was damaged against the guardrail, the other broke its gearbox.

With Wollek's Lancia delayed, Henri Pescarolo and Klaus Ludwig took the lead for Joest's Porsche team, which was down to one car after Stefan Johansson slid on oil and damaged his 956 during the night. In pursuit was Preston Henn's brand-new black Porsche driven by John Paul Junior and Jean Rondeau (Henn himself drove for an hour), and the Kremer team's best Porsche driven by Alan Jones/Vern Schuppan/Jean-Pierre Jarier.

The racing was still close, Pescarolo losing the lead briefly when a suspension upright had to be changed, then forging ahead again, but the Kremer team dropped to sixth when a piston failed in the last hour. The result was another crushing display for Porsche, even without factory cars, the customers claiming the top seven places, and ninth.

The advertised tightening of fuel restrictions was implemented in 1985, reducing the allocation to 510 litres for 1,000 km events and from 2,600 litres to 2,210 for Le Mans, and ironically, in view of its boycott of Le Mans the year before, the Rothmans team seemed to be hardest hit. In the races leading up to Le Mans the works cars were strangely subdued, the engineers failing to find the electronic microchip that would give speed with fuel economy, and clearly there

Two customer Porsches provided the leading duel in 1985, Richard Lloyd's Canon sponsored 956 driven by Jonathan Palmer and James Weaver, Reinhold Joest's New Man sponsored car by Klaus Ludwig, Paolo Barilla and 'John Winter' (Porsche).

was no improvement when the works cars prepared for the 24-Hours.

They were quick in practice, of course, when there is no need for economy. Hans Stuck became the first man to break the 250 km/h (155 mph) barrier in his Rothmans-Porsche 962C, shared with Derek Bell, lapping in 3 min 14.8 sec for an average of 251.815 km/h (156.48 mph). This year the works team ran the 962C chassis, a longer wheelbase version of the 956 developed for the IMSA series, and had new 3-litre, fully water–cooled engines installed for practice only, with a reputed 700 bhp. In the race though they relied on the usual 2.6 litre engines, like the customer teams, while Lancia continued to rely upon their full 3-litre V8 power units.

With the accent on economy the race looked a sleepy affair, viewed from the pits. The drivers were keeping their revs down, changing gear with deliberate care, and after leading the race for four laps Wollek deliberately pulled to one side on the straight and let four Porsches go by. Stuck drifted down to twelfth place, Ickx to twenty-first position. It hardly seemed like a race . . . but viewed from the Mulsanne Straight it was another matter, the Porsches and Lancias blasting down the 3.5 mile highway at up to 370 km/h (230 mph). That is a truly inspiring sight!

Reinhold Joest's number 7 Porsche driven by Klaus Ludwig, Paolo Barilla and 'John Winter' pitched a battle with Richard Lloyd's Canon–sponsored Porsche driven by Jonathan Palmer and James Weaver, and the race was theirs. Ludwig and Palmer slipstreamed through the first two hours, the two drivers established a rapport

Reinhold Joest's famous Porsche 956/117 won the Le Mans race in 1984 and again in 1985 after text-book runs. In 1984 Henri Pescarolo co-drove with Klaus Ludwig, and in 1985 Ludwig was assisted by Paolo Barilla and 'John Winter' (Porsche).

which enabled them both to save fuel. Ickx was badly delayed by a gearbox rebuild, the oil cooler not having been tightened up properly before the race, and the Canon-Porsche then lost a lap when the engine misfired, and an adjustment was carried out on the Motronic management box. The third Rothmans-Porsche of Al Holbert, Vern Schuppan and John Watson had moved into second place at half distance, the Brun Motorsport-Porsche was third, Wollek's Lancia fourth and the Canon-Porsche fifth, Stuck and Bell dropping back with a wheel bearing failure, then another. Later the crankshaft was to break in Watson's works Porsche — only the second engine failure suffered by the works team in three seasons — and Ludwig, Barilla and 'Winter' were under no threat as they reeled out a three-lap victory over Palmer, Weaver, and Richard Lloyd who drove for an hour. Bell and Stuck salvaged third place, lapping faster on Sunday with a new Motronic microchip, and fourth and fifth were the John Fitzpatrick Racing and Kremer Porsche Racing entries.

The Lancias faded to sixth and seventh positions, with several minor problems but none worse than a broken turbocharger, which delayed Wollek's car half an hour, while the Group 44 Jaguars failed to make much impression. One retired in the night with a broken driveshaft constant velocity joint, and Tullius's barely made it to the finish, in thirteenth place, with a broken piston.

The Lancias were pulled out of the Group C championship at the end of the season, after beating the Rothmans team for the first, and only, time in the shortened race at Spa in September. That day Stefan Bellof lost his life at Eau Rouge, in a suicidal attempt to pass Jacky Ickx, and the Belgian retired, finally, from racing at the end of the season. His record of six Le Mans victories between 1969 and 1982 may stand for a long time, and in his wake fellow Belgian Olivier Gendebien, and Frenchman Henri Pescarolo, each had four successes.

Derek Bell would raise his score to five Le Mans victories, Al Holbert to four, and Hans Stuck to two, by winning the classic event in 1986 and in 1987. They, with Porsche, were well into the winning groove, and the 1986 race was enjoyed, for nearly 12 hours, as the Rothmans and Joest teams duelled without let-up. Bell/Stuck/Holbert and Ludwig/Barilla/'Winter' were rarely out of each other's sight through the evening, and in the darkest hours of the night, racing away from the field. Mass, Wollek and Schuppan were up there, too, until Mass slid off after hitting an oil slick, the German's luck at the Sarthe never improving . . .

Jaguar returned to Le Mans in 1985 represented by Bob Tullius's Group 44 team from America. The Brian Redman/ Hurley Haywood/Jim Adam XJR-5 failed to finish, but Tullius/Chip Robinson/Claud Ballot-Lena limped home thirteenth and won the GTP category (Jaguar).

Jaguar was represented by three Tom Walkinshaw Racing, Silk Cut cigarette–sponsored XJR-6 models, all powered by the V12 production engine, and they were rather more effective than the IMSA Jaguars had been. One ran out of fuel on the circuit, however, and another had a broken driveshaft cv joint in the night, leaving one Coventry Cat to keep tabs on the leaders.

The race crumbled in misery when Jo Gartner lost control of his

Derek Bell became the most successful British driver in the race's history when he achieved his fourth victory in 1986. The works Rothmans-Porsche 962C was co-driven by Hans Stuck and Al Holbert (Porsche).

Kremer Porsche shortly before four o'clock in the morning, the car unaccountably turning left on the straight and flattening a barrier before hitting a telegraph pole. The popular Austrian was killed instantly, and here was yet another shocking accident of the sort that all the professional drivers feared.

While running behind the pace cars at reduced speed, Ludwig's engine ran its bearings and the German vowed, as he changed his kit, never to race again at Le Mans, though an offer from the Porsche factory in 1988 was too good to refuse! Still the surviving Jaguar might have been second, had not a rear tyre burst on the Mulsanne mid-morning on Sunday. Both the Mercedes V8 powered Saubers had gone home early after running into engine problems, and Porsches claimed the top seven positions. Could they ever be beaten?

Tom Walkinshaw prepared his best-ever effort for 1987, bringing three highly–developed XJR-8 models to Le Mans, each tested as thoroughly as possible. Some people even reckoned they were the favourites, after beating the Rothmans-Porsche team four times consecutively in the opening rounds of the 1987 championship, and the odds in their favour lengthened when Price Cobb wrote-off a Rothmans Porsche during qualifying, and Mass's engine broke within the first hour of the race.

New regulations required the Group C cars to run on commercial grade fuel, without special additives which were good for the turbocharged engines, and the Porsche teams had suffered in

Grim expressions in the Silk Cut Jaguar pit after Schlesser comes in with a burst tyre. The ensuing damage is too serious to repair (Jaguar).

consequence. Even so, it was a major surprise to see the top private teams of Joest and Kremer dropping out within 30 minutes of the start of the race, inevitably blaming their Motronic systems for weakening the mixtures and causing piston damage.

Two Porsches only remained in contention, those of Bell/Stuck/Holbert and the Richard Lloyd, Liqui Moly–sponsored entry of Jonathan Palmer/James Weaver/Price Cobb, and the British entry was going well until an oil line broke, and the car caught fire in the night. One works Porsche versus three strong Jaguars suggested a

victory for Jaguar, one that would suitably celebrate the thirtieth anniversary of the company's last success.

In the eleventh hour Win Percy crashed his Jaguar at top speed on the Mulsanne Straight, yet another victim of a catastrophic tyre failure. Jaguar, like Porsche, had sensors to warn the drivers of impending tyre problems, but rain early in the race had rendered these useless and Percy was a lucky passenger as his XJR-8 destroyed itself, without harming him.

The solo Porsche led through the night, but only narrowly, and at

A trio of Jaguars prepared by Tom Walkinshaw contested the 24-Hour race in 1986, but none finished. Eddie Cheever, Derek Warwick and Jean-Louis Schlesser remained in contention until Sunday morning, when a burst tyre wrecked their chances (Jaguar).

breakfast time on Sunday Jaguar's hopes evaporated. Martin Brundle retired his car from second place with a cracked cylinder head, and he was followed in by Eddie Cheever whose gearbox had broken. That could be repaired in time, but a faulty wheel bearing further delayed the Jaguar and Walkinshaw's team had to settle for fifth place, vowing to return in 1988 to settle the issue.

The 1987 results had a rather different look. Second, but 20 laps behind, was the Primagaz-sponsored Porsche of Pierre Yver/Jürgen Lassig/Bernard de Dryver and third, the same team's Porsche 962 powered Cougar driven by constructor Yves Courage — the Porsche dealer in Le Mans — Pierre-Henri Raphanel and Hervé Regout.

Nissan, Toyota and Mazda all had entries, but the Japanese manufacturers were not yet in a position to contest the lead. Mazda had the only finisher, a rotary powered 757 in seventh place, but it is expected that the three manufacturers will step up their efforts in the years to come.

The Porsche era ended in 1987, though surely the Stuttgart manufacturer will return soon enough to claim new prestige. In retrospect, the Rothmans-Porsche driven by Derek Bell, Hans Stuck and Al Holbert did more than one might have expected, fending off a massive Jaguar attack for hour after hour, wearing down and eventually destroying the British challenge.

Porsche's team took victory with honour in 1987, and defeat with pride a year later. At last Jaguar's enormous investment did pay off as the Gallahers Silk Cut sponsored XJR-9LM driven by Jan Lammers, Johnny Dumfries and Andy Wallace claimed an outstanding victory, at an average speed far higher than had been recorded for many years, regardless of the circuit's configuration.

The long straight from Le Mans to Mulsanne had been resurfaced to a very high standard, and the quickest cars were now running consistently at up to 390 km/h (242 mph). The WM-Peugeot team, in fact, took 'Projet Quatre Cents' to the Sarthe for the second time and achieved its objective, having the car timed at 405 km/h (251.65 mph) during the course of the race!

The higher speeds led to unexpected tyre problems for both Jaguar and Sauber Mercedes during the first evening of qualifying (the test weekend had been cancelled because of the resurfacing work), and intense discussion in Peter Sauber's camp led to the decision to withdraw from the race. Once again, Jaguar would be the prime challengers to Porsche, the German team being absent from the World Championship but preparing in depth for this one event.

Klaus Ludwig joned Bell and Stuck in the 'lead' Porsche, Ludwig unfortunately driving half of one lap very slowly indeed early in the race, trying to make one lap too many on the fuel available. Lammers' Jaguar was running at or near the front throughout the 24 hours, the other four Jaguars not finding quite the same pace, though Martin Brundle and John Nielsen believed they had a chance until their engine failed on Sunday.

Two of the three works Porsches failed too, Bob Wollek's with an engine failure and the Andretti family's slowing towards the end with one cylinder out of action. The Jaguar team became increasingly nervous as the end neared, but Lammers and crew kept the number 2 XJR going beautifully to the finish, merely 2½ minutes ahead of Bell, Stuck and Ludwig. It was a memorable race by any yardstick, the kind of episode that makes the 24-Hours of Le Mans famous.

From gravel to tarmac . . . from open four-seater touring cars to closed, cockpit projectiles capable of travelling faster than light aircraft . . . that is the story of development at Le Mans, the postwar era bringing a new breed of car so fast that eventually even the drivers grew afraid of their energy.

The circuit did not develop as quickly as the cars that raced on it, that is certain. The pit area was open and dangerous until 1970, and in 1987 some of the armco railing along the Mulsanne Straight was far from secure, pathetically inadequate to contain a wayward car travelling at 230 mph. But what could the Automobile Club de l'Ouest do, and the Departement de Sarthe? The Porsche 917s also covered the ground at 230 mph, and then there were trees alongside the road, before armco. It is not a permanent race track, but a public highway for 360 days of the year, and in truth the cars themselves had outstripped the safety facilities.

The professional drivers muttered among themselves, talked of boycotts, decisions of conscience, but FISA paid only lip service to the need to slow the cars down. In 1976 the ACO decided that Group 5, production-based cars on their own would not be attractive to the crowds, and actually forced the pace of Group 6 sportscar development. Now, it seems, there is no turning back.

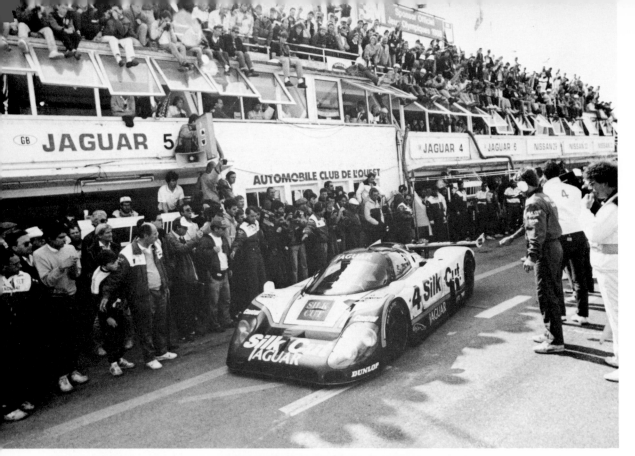

Above *Jaguar's XJR-8LM team ran very strongly in 1987 and seemed to have a good chance of winning, until 8 am on Sunday when the two surviving cars had mechanical problems. Cheever leaves the pits after a gearbox repair (Jaguar).*

Right *Yet another victory for the Rothmans-Porsche team, for the second year running in a 962C driven by Bell, Stuck and Holbert in 1987. Theirs was the only works car to survive the first hour of the race, but it ran faultlessly (Porsche).*

Right *Jaguar's determined bid to win again at Le Mans finally paid off in 1988 when Jan Lammers, Johnny Dumfries and Andy Wallace claimed the honour in their XJR-9LM, beating the works Porsche of Hans Stuck, Derek Bell and Klaus Ludwig by just half a lap.*

Right *Jacky Ickx (Belgium), six times winner at Le Mans.*

Right *Derek Bell (Great Britain), five times winner (Rothmans).*

Above *Henri Pescarolo (France), four times winner.*

Above middle *Olivier Gendebien (Belgium), four times winner.*

Above right *Al Holbert (USA), three times winner.*

Right *Klaus Ludwig (Germany), three times winner.*

Appendix I

Le Mans winners, 1923–88

Circuit: 17.262 km (10.726 miles)

1923 André Lagache/René Leonard (3.0 Chenard & Walcker), 2,209.5 km (1,372.9 miles) at 92.06 km/h (57.2 mph).
Fastest lap: Frank Clement (3.0 Bentley), 9 min 39 sec, 107.32 km/h (66.69 mph).
Starters: 33. Finishers: 30.

1924 John Duff/Frank Clement (3.0 Bentley), 2,077.3 km (1,290.79 miles) at 86.55 km/h (53.78 mph).
Fastest lap: André Lagache (4.0 La Lorraine), 9 min 19 sec, 111.16 km/h (69.07 mph).
Starters: 40. Finishers: 14.

1925 Gérard de Courcelles/André Rossignol (3.5 La Lorraine), 2,233.98 km (1,388.12 miles) at 93.08 km/h (57.83 mph).
Fastest lap: André Lagache (4.0 Chenard & Walcker), 9 min 10 sec, 112.98 km/h (70.20 mph).
Starters: 49. Finishers: 16.

1926 Robert Bloch/André Rossignol (3.5 La Lorraine), 2,552.4 km (1,585.99 miles) at 106.35 km/h (66.08 mph).
Fastest lap: Gérard de Courcelles (3.5 La Lorraine), 9 min 3 sec, 114.44 km/h (71.12 mph).

1927 J. Dudley Benjafield/Sammy Davis (3.0 Bentley), 2,369.8 km (1,472.5 miles) at 98.74 km/h (61.35 mph).
Fastest lap: Frank Clement (4.4 Bentley), 8 min 46 sec, 118.14 km/h (73.41 mph).
Starters: 22. Finishers: 7.

1928 Woolf Barnato/Bernard Rubin (4.4 Bentley), 2,669.1 km (1,658.6 miles) at 111.21 km/h (69.10 mph).
Fastest lap: Tim Birkin (4.4 Bentley), 8 min 7 sec, 127.60 km/h (79.23 mph).
Starters: 33. Finishers: 17.

Circuit: 16.34 km (10.153 miles)

1929 Woolf Barnato/Tim Birkin (6.6 Bentley), 2,843.83 km (1,767.07 miles) at 118.49 km/h (73.62 mph).
Fastest lap: Birkin, 7 min 21 sec, 133.55 km/h (82.98 mph).
Starters: 25. Finishers: 10.

1930 Woolf Barnato/Glen Kidston (6.6. Bentley), 2,930.66 km (1,821.02 miles) at 122.11 km/h (75.87 mph).
Fastest lap: Tim Birkin (4.4 Bentley), 6 min 48 sec, 144.36 km/h (89.69 mph).
Starters: 17. Finishers: 9.

1931 Earl Howe/Tim Birkin (2.3 s/c Alfa Romeo 8C), 3,017.65 km (1,875.07 miles) at 125.73 km/h (78.12 mph).
Fastest lap: B. Ivanowski (7.1 s/c Mercedes SSK), 7 min 3 sec, 139.24 km/h (86.51 mph).
Starters: 26. Finishers: 6.

Circuit: 13.492 km (8.384 miles)

1932 Raymond Sommer/Luigi Chinetti (2.3 s/c Alfa Romeo 8C), 2,954.08 km (1,835.55 miles) at 123.08 km/h (76.48 mph).
Fastest lap: M. Minoia (2.3 s/c Alfa Romeo 8C), 5 min 41 sec, 142.43 km/h (88.50 mph).
Starters: 26. Finishers: 9.

1933 Raymond Sommer/Tazio Nuvolari (2.3 s/c Alfa Romeo 8C), 3,144.03 km (1,953.61 miles) at 131.0 km/h (81.4 mph).
Fastest lap: Sommer, 5 min 38.8 sec, 146.38 km/h (90.96 mph).
Starters: 29. Finishers: 13.

1934 Luigi Chinetti/Philippe Etancelin (2.3 s/c Alfa Romeo 8C), 2,886.93 km (1,793.85 miles) at 120.289 km/h (74.74 mph).
Fastest lap: Etancelin, 5 min 41 sec, 142.43 km/h (88.5 mph).
Starters: 44. Finishers: 23.

1935 John Hindmarsh/Louis Fontés (4.4 Lagonda M45R), 3,006.79 km (1,868.3 miles) at 125.28 km/h (77.84 mph).
Fastest lap: Earl Howe (2.3 s/c Alfa Romeo 8), 5 min 47.9 sec, 139.61 km/h (86.75 mph).
Starters: 58. Finishers: 28.

1936 Race cancelled (due to strikes).

1937   Jean-Pierre Wimille/Robert Benoist (3.3 Bugatti 57S), 3,287.93 km
(2,043.0 miles) at 136.99 km/h (85.12 mph).
Fastest lap: Wimille, 5 min 13 sec, 155.17 km/h (96.42 mph).
Starters: 48. Finishers: 17.

1938   Eugene Chaboud/Jean Tremoulet (3.6 Delahaye 135M), 3,180.94 km
(1,976.54 miles) at 132.53 km/h (82.35 mph).
Fastest lap: Raymond Sommer (2.9 s/c Alfa Romeo 8C), 5 min 13.8 sec,
154.78 km/h (96.17 mph).
Starters: 42. Finishers: 15.

1939   Jean-Pierre Wimille/Pierre Veyron (3.3 s/c Bugatti 57C), 3,354.76 km
(2,084.54 miles) at 139.78 km/h (86.55 mph).
Fastest lap: Raymond Mazaud (3.6 Delahaye 135M), 5 min 12.1 sec, 155.62
km/h (96.74 mph).
Starters: 42. Finishers: 20.

1940-   Races cancelled.
1948

1949   Luigi Chinetti/Lord Selsdon (2.0 Ferrari 166M), 3,178.29 km (1,974.89
miles) at 132.42 km/h (82.28 mph).
Fastest lap: André Simon (4.5 Delahaye), 5 min 12.5 sec, 155.42 km/h
(96.57 mph).
Starters: 49. Finishers: 19.

1950   Louis Rosier/Jean-Louis Rosier (4.5 Talbot-Lago), 3,465.12 km (2,153.12
miles) at 144.38 km/h (89.71 mph).
Fastest lap: Louis Rosier, 4 min 53.5 sec, 165.49 km/h (102.84 mph).
Starters: 60. Finishers: 29.

1951   Peter Walker/Peter Whitehead (3.4 Jaguar XK120C), 3,611.19 km
(2,243.88 miles) at 150.46 km/h (93.49 mph).
Fastest lap: Stirling Moss (3.4 Jaguar XK120C), 4 min 46.8 sec, 169.35
km/h (105.24 mph).
Starters: 60. Finishers: 30.

1952   Hermann Lang/Fritz Reiss (3.0 Mercedes 300SL), 3,733.8 km (2,320.07
miles) at 155.57 km/h (96.69 mph).
Fastest lap: Alberto Ascari (3.0 Ferrari 250S), 4 min 40.5 sec, 173.15 km/h
(107.59 mph).
Starters: 57. Finishers: 17.

1953   Tony Rolt/Duncan Hamilton (3.4 Jaguar C-type), 4,088.06 km (2,540.2
miles) at 170.336 km/h (105.84 mph).
Fastest lap: Alberto Ascari (4.5 Ferrari 375 MM), 4 min 27.4 sec, 181.64
km/h (112.85 mph).
Starters: 60. Finishers: 26.

1954   Froilan Gonzalez/Maurice Trintignant (5.0 Ferrari 375), 4,061.15 km
(2,523.47 miles) at 169.21 km/h (105.14 mph).
Fastest lap: G. Marzotto (5.0 Ferrari 375), 4 min 16.8 sec, 189.13 km/h
(117.53 mph).
Starters: 57. Finishers: 18.

1955   Mike Hawthorn/Ivor Bueb (3.4 Jaguar D-type), 4,135.38 km (2,569.6 miles)
at 172.3 km/h (107.06 mph).
Fastest lap: Hawthorn, 4 min 6.6 sec, 196.96 km/h (122.39 mph).
Starters: 60. Finishers: 21.

Circuit: 13.461 km (8.364 miles)

1956   Ron Flockhart/Ninian Sanderson (3.4 Jaguar D-type), 4,034.92 km
(2,507.18 miles) at 168.12 km/h (104.46 mph).
Fastest lap: Mike Hawthorn (3.4 Jaguar D-type), 4 min 20.0 sec, 186.38
km/h (115.82 mph).
Starters: 49. Finishers: 14.

1957   Ron Flockhart/Ivor Bueb (3.8 Jaguar D-type), 4,397.1 km (2,732.23 miles)
at 183.21 km/h (113.84 mph).
Fastest lap: Mike Hawthorn (4.0 Ferrari 412), 3 min 58.7 sec, 203.01 km/h
(126.14 mph).
Starters: 54. Finishers: 20.

1958   Olivier Gendebien/Phil Hill (3.0 Ferrari 250TR), 4,101.92 km (2,548.81
miles) at 170.91 km/h (106.20 mph).
Fastest lap: Mike Hawthorn (3.0 Ferrari 250TR), 4 min 8.0 sec, 195.40
km/h (121.32 mph).
Starters: 55. Finishers: 20.

1959   Carroll Shelby/Roy Salvadori (3.0 Aston Martin DBR1), 4,347.90 km
(2,701.65 miles) at 181.16 km/h (112.56 mph).
Fastest lap: Jean Behra (3.0 Ferrari 250TR), 4 min 0.9 sec, 201.16 km/h
(125.0 mph).
Starters: 53. Finishers: 13.

1960   Olivier Gendebien/Paul Frère (3.0 Ferrari TR60), 4,217.52 km (2,620.64
miles) at 175.73 km/h (109.19 mph).
Fastest lap: Masten Gregory (2.9 Maserati T61), 4 min 4.0 sec, 195.60
km/h (121.54 mph).
Starters: 55. Finishers: 20.

1961   Olivier Gendebien/Phil Hill (3.0 Ferrari TR61), 4,476.58 km (2,781.61
miles) at 186.52 km/h (115.90 mph).
Fastest lap: Ricardo Rodriguez (3.0 Ferrari TR61), 3 min 59.09 sec, 201.20
km/h (125.40 mph).
Starters: 55. Finishers: 22.

1962   Olivier Gendebien/Phil Hill (4.0 Ferrari 330LM), 4,451.25 km (2,765.87
miles) at 185.46 km/h (115.24 mph).
Fastest lap: Phil Hill, 3 min 57.3 sec, 204.20 km/h (126.89 mph).
Starters: 55. Finishers: 18.

1963 Lodovico Scarfiotti/Lorenzo Bandini (3.0 Ferrari 250P), 4,561.71 km (2,834.50 miles) at 190.07 km/h (118.1 mph).
Fastest lap: John Surtees (3.0 Ferrari 250P), 3 min 53.3 sec, 207.71 km/h (129.07 mph).
Starters: 49. Finishers: 12.

1964 Jean Guichet/Nino Vaccarella (3.3 Ferrari 275P), 4,695.31 km (2,917.52 miles) at 195.63 km/h (121.56 mph).
Fastest lap: Phil Hill (4.2 Ford GT40), 3 min 49.2 sec, 211.42 km/h (131.37 mph).
Starters: 55. Finishers: 24.

1965 Jochen Rindt/Masten Gregory (3.3 Ferrari 275LM), 4,677.01 km (2,906.21 miles) at 194.88 km/h (121.09 mph).
Fastest lap: Phil Hill (7.0 Ford Mk2), 3 min 37.5 sec, 222.80 km/h (138.44 mph).
Starters: 51. Finishers: 14.

1966 Bruce McLaren/Chris Amon (7.0 Ford Mk2), 4,843.08 km (3,009.35 miles) at 201.79 km/h (125.38 mph).
Fastest lap: Dan Gurney (7.0 Ford Mk2), 3 min 30.6 sec, 230.10 km/h (142.97 mph).
Starters: 55. Finishers: 15.

1967 Dan Gurney/A. J. Foyt (7.0 Ford Mk4), 5,232.90 km (3,251.72 miles) at 218.03 km/h (135.48 mph).
Fastest lap: Denny Hulme and Mario Andretti (both in 7.0 Ford Mk4), 3 min 23.6 sec, 238.01 km/h (147.89 mph).
Starters: 54. Finishers: 16.

Circuit: 13.469 km (8.369 miles)

1968 Pedro Rodriguez/Lucien Bianchi (5.0 Ford GT40), 4,452.88 km (2,766.88 miles) at 185.53 km/h (115.28 mph).
Fastest lap: Rolf Stommelen (3.0 Porsche 908), 3 min 38.1 sec, 222.23 km/h (138.14 mph).
Starters: 54. Finishers: 15.

1969 Jacky Ickx/Jack Oliver (5.0 Ford GT40), 4,998.0 km (3,105.5 miles) at 208.25 km/h (129.40 mph).
Fastest lap: Vic Elford (4.5 Porsche 917), 3 min 27.2 sec, 234.01 km/h (145.41 mph).
Starters: 45. Finishers: 14.

1970 Hans Herrmann/Richard Attwood (4.5 Porsche 917), 4,607.81 km (2,863.15 miles) at 191.99 km/h (119.29 mph).
Fastest lap: Vic Elford (4.9 Porsche 917), 3 min 21.0 sec, 241.235 km/h (149.89 mph).
Starters: 51. Finishers: 7.

1971 Helmuth Marko/Gijs van Lennep (4.9 Porsche 917), 5,335.31 km (3,315.20 miles) at 222.30 km/h (138.13 mph).
Fastest lap: Jack Oliver and Pedro Rodriguez (both 4.9 Porsche 917), 3 min 18.4 sec, 244.38 km/h (151.85 mph).
Starters: 49. Finishers: 13.

Circuit: 13.64 km (8.475 miles)

1972 Henri Pescarolo/Graham Hill (3.0 Matra MS670), 4,691.34 km (2,915.05 miles) at 195.47 km/h (121.45 mph).
Fastest lap: Gijs van Lennep (3.0 Lola DFV T280), 3 min 46.9 sec, 216.41 km/h (134.47 mph).
Starters: 55. Finishers: 18.

1973 Henri Pescarolo/Gérard Larrousse (3.0 Matra MS670B), 4,853.94 km (3,016.09 miles) at 202.24 km/h (125.67 mph).
Fastest lap: François Cevert (3.0 Matra MS670B), 3 min 39.6 sec, 223.6 km/h (138.94 mph).
Starters: 55. Finishers: 21.

1974 Henri Pescarolo/Gérard Larrousse (3.0 Matra MS670B), 4,606.57 km (2,862.38 miles) at 191.94 km/h (119.26 mph).
Fastest lap: Jean-Pierre Jarier (3.0 Matra MS680), 3 min 42.7 sec, 220.49 km/h (137.01 mph).
Starters: 49. Finishers: 19.

1975 Jacky Ickx/Derek Bell (3.0 Gulf-Mirage DFV GR8), 4,595.57 km (2,855.55 miles) at 191.48 km/h (118.98 mph).
Fastest lap: Chris Craft (3.0 De Cadenet Lola DFV T380), 3 min 53.8 sec, 210.02 km/h (130.50 mph).
Starters: 55. Finishers: 31.

1976 Jacky Ickx/Gijs van Lennep (2.1 t/c Porsche 936), 4,769.92 km (2,963.88 miles) at 198.74 km/h (123.49 mph).
Fastest lap: Jean-Pierre Jabouille (2.0 t/c Renault-Alpine A442), 3 min 43.0 sec, 220.19 km/h (136.91 mph).
Starters: 55. Finishers: 27.

1977 Jacky Ickx/Hurley Haywood/Jürgen Barth (2.1 t/c Porsche 936), 4,671.63 km (2,902.81 miles) at 194.65 km/h (120.95 mph).
Fastest lap: Ickx, 3 min 36.5 sec, 226.80 km/h (140.93 mph).
Starters: 55. Finishers: 21.

1978 Jean-Pierre Jaussaud/Didier Pironi (2.0 t/c Renault-Alpine A442), 5,044.53 km (3,134.51 miles), at 210.18 km/h (130.6 mph).
Fastest lap: Jean-Pierre Jabouille (2.0 t/c Renault-Alpine A442), 3 min 34.2 sec, 229.24 km/h (142.44 mph).
Starters: 55. Finishers: 17.

Circuit: 13.626 km (8.467 miles)

1979 Klaus Ludwig/Bill Whittington/Don Whittington (2.8 t/c Porsche 935), 4,173.93 km (2,590.93 miles) at 173.91 km/h (108.1 mph).
Fastest lap: Jacky Ickx (2.1 t/c Porsche 936), 3 min 36.1 sec, 227.0 km/h (141.05 mph).
Starters: 55. Finishers: 22.

1980 Jean Rondeau/Jean-Pierre Jaussaud (3.0 Rondeau-DFV M379B), 4,608.02 km (2,861.40 miles) at 192.00 km/h (119.22 mph).
Fastest lap: Jacky Ickx (2.1 t/c Porsche 936), 3 min 40.6 sec, 222.36 km/h (138.17 mph).
Starters: 55. Finishers: 25.

1981   Jacky Ickx/Derek Bell (2.6 t/c Porsche 936), 4,825.34 km (2,998.33 miles) at 201.05 km/h (124.93 mph).
Fastest lap: Hurley Haywood (2.6 t/c Porsche 936), 3 min 33.5 sec, 229.23 km/h (142.44 mph).
Starters: 55. Finishers: 21.

1982   Jacky Ickx/Derek Bell (2.6 t/c Porsche 956), 4,899.08 km (3,044.15 miles) at 204.12 km/h (126.84 mph).
Fastest lap: Jean Ragnotti (3.9 Rondeau-DFL M382), 3 min 36.5 sec, 226.15 km/h (140.53 mph).
Starters: 55. Finishers: 19.

1983   Vern Schuppan/Al Holbert/Hurley Haywood (2.6 t/c Porsche 956), 5,047.93 km (3,136.45 miles) at 210.33 km/h (130.69 mph).
Fastest lap: Jacky Ickx (2.6 t/c Porsche 956), 3 min 29.7 sec, 233.92 km/h (145.35 mph).
Starters: 51. Finishers: 21.

1984   Klaus Ludwig/Henri Pescarolo (2.6 t/c Porsche 956), 4,900.27 km (3,045.3 miles) at 204.17 km/h (126.88 mph).
Fastest lap: Alessandro Nannini (2.8 t/c Lancia LC2), 3 min 28.9 sec, 234.82 km/h (145.86 mph).
Starters: 53. Finishers: 22.

1985   Klaus Ludwig/Paolo Barilla/'John Winter' (2.6 t/c Porsche 956), 5,088.50 km (3,161.84 miles) at 212.01 km/h (131.94 mph).
Fastest lap: Jochen Mass (2.6 t/c Porsche 962C), 3 min 25.1 sec, 239.55 km/h (148.61 mph).
Starters: 49. Finishers: 29.

Circuit: 13.52 km (8.401 miles)

1986   Derek Bell/Hans Stuck/Al Holbert (3.0 t/c Porsche 962C), 4,972.73 km (3,089.90 miles) at 207.19 km/h (128.74 mph).
Fastest lap: Klaus Ludwig (2.6 t/c Porsche 956), 3 min 23.2 sec, 239.55 km/h (148.82 mph).
Starters: 50. Finishers: 19.

Circuit: 13.535 km (8.411 miles)

1987   Derek Bell/Hans Stuck/Al Holbert (3.0 t/c Porsche 962C), 4,791.77 km (2,977.60 miles) at 199.65 km/h (124.06 mph).
Fastest lap: Johnny Dumfries (5.0 t/c Sauber Mercedes C9), 3 min 25.4 sec, 237.22 km/h (147.41 mph).
Starters: 47. Finishers: 12.

1988   Jan Lammers/Johnny Dumfries/Andy Wallace (7.0 Jaguar XJR-9LM), 5,332.79 km (3,313.69 miles) at 221.665 km/h (137.74 mph).
Fastest lap: Hans Stuck (3.0 t/c Porsche 962C), 3 min 22.50 sec, 240.662 km/h (149.52 mph).
Starters: 49. Finishers: 25.

Appendix II

The Le Mans circuit: the major changes since 1923

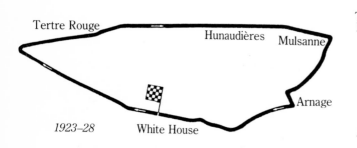

1923–28

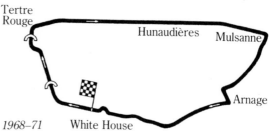

1968–71

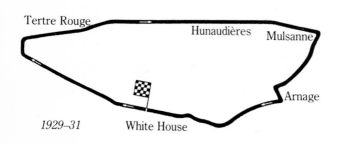

1929–31

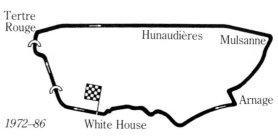

1972–86

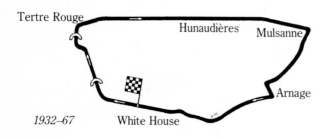

1932–67

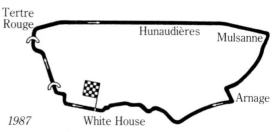

1987

Index